THE LIFE OF
PENNSYLVANIA
GOVERNOR
GEORGE M. LEADER

THE LIFE OF PENNSYLVANIA GOVERNOR GEORGE M. LEADER

Challenging Complacency

Kenneth C. Wolensky
with
George M. Leader

Lehigh University Press
Bethlehem

Published by Lehigh University Press
Co-published with The Rowman & Littlefield Publishing Group, Inc.
4501 Forbes Boulevard, Suite 200, Lanham, Maryland 20706
www.rowmanlittlefield.com

Estover Road, Plymouth PL6 7PY, United Kingdom

Copyright © 2011 by Kenneth C. Wolensky

All rights reserved. No part of this book may be reproduced in any form or by any electronic or mechanical means, including information storage and retrieval systems, without written permission from the publisher, except by a reviewer who may quote passages in a review.

British Library Cataloguing in Publication Information Available

Library of Congress Cataloging-in-Publication Data

Wolensky, Kenneth C.
 The life of Pennsylvania Governor George M. Leader : challenging complacency / Kenneth C. Wolensky, with George M. Leader.
     p. cm.
 "Co-published with the Rowman & Littlefield Publishing Group, Inc."
 ISBN 978-1-61146-079-7 (cloth : alk. paper) — ISBN 978-1-61146-080-3 (ebook)
 1. Leader, George M., 1918- 2. Governors—Pennsylvania—Biography.
 3. Pennsylvania—Politics and government—1951- I. Leader, George M., 1918- II. Title.
   F155.3.L43W65 2011
   974.8'043092—dc23
   [B]
                                                                    2011020645

∞^{TM} The paper used in this publication meets the minimum requirements of American National Standard for Information Sciences—Permanence of Paper for Printed Library Materials, ANSI/NISO Z39.48-1992.

Printed in the United States of America

Contents

Introduction   1

1   Early Years, Parents, and Family   9

2   World War II and Early Political Ventures   35

3   The Keystone State's Chief Executive, 1955–1959   51

4   The 1958 U.S. Senate Campaign and Postgubernatorial Years   101

5   Wellness, Faith, and Family   119

6   Views, Philosophies, and Ideas about Contemporary Issues   137

7   The Humanitarian   155

Epilogue   171

Appendix A   George M. Leader Family Library and Archives, Master List and Finding Aid   179

Appendix B Manuscript Group 207
            State Archives of Pennsylvania
            Pennsylvania Historical and Museum
              Commission
            George M. Leader Papers   183

Index   185

About the Author   189

Introduction

He stands among Pennsylvania's very few and quickly dwindling public officials who have held office and political sway in the mid-twentieth century. When research for this biography commenced, former U.S. Congressman and Governor William W. Scranton (1963–1967) and George Michael Leader (1955–1959) were the only living governors from the mid-twentieth century. They both date to an era long gone in Pennsylvania politics. Handshakes secured votes. Candidates got to know the electorate by greeting them at county fairs and on street corners. Stump speeches were common. Personal attacks targeted at opponents were few. Campaigning was done mostly without television advertising and, if the media was used, small campaign budgets kept its use in check. Leader, in fact, was the first gubernatorial candidate to use TV, albeit on a very small budget.

George Leader was an influential public official in that era. He was born on January 17, 1918, in York County, Pennsylvania, the son of Guy A. and Beulah (Boyer) Leader. Like his Pennsylvania German family that had farmed in York County for several generations, the future governor of Pennsylvania both grew up and worked on his parent's poultry farm. He attended a one-room schoolhouse and York High School. He graduated in 1939 from Gettysburg College. Then, with his new bride Mary Jane Strickler, he attended the University of Pennsylvania, where he studied public administration, philosophy, and economics at the Fells Institute of Local and State Government.

During World War II, Leader served as a Navy ensign responsible for ship and crew supplies on the aircraft carrier USS *Randolph*, where he earned the rank of full lieutenant. At the end of the war he returned to York, purchased Willow Brook Farm, and launched a political career as secretary, and later as chair, of the York County Democratic Committee. Like his father, George became a hatchery man and an activist in Democratic Party politics. In the 1940s Guy Leader was a state senator representing the 28th district. In 1950 George ran for and won his father's seat when the elder Leader stepped down. Two years later he unsuccessfully ran for state treasurer. Undeterred by the loss, he then launched a candidacy for the governor's office. According to Leader, upon learning of Leader's candidacy, former Philadelphia mayor and U.S. Senator Joseph Clark quipped, "I'm sorry to hear it. George Leader is a nice fellow. I hate to see him be the sacrificial lamb."

Clark knew that, historically, it was rather unusual for candidates from the party of Thomas Jefferson, Andrew Jackson, and Franklin Delano Roosevelt to succeed in a gubernatorial race in the Keystone State. With the exception of George Earle (1935–1939), no Democrat had claimed the title in the twentieth century. Leader, however, is not one to be underestimated nor is he one to be reticent about issues in which he believes. He campaigned vigorously and was among the pioneering candidates who utilized media advertising and professional pollsters. With agrarian and labor support, George Leader defeated his opponent Lloyd Wood by 280,000 votes. It was an upset. At 36 years old, George Leader was the second youngest person ever elected as governor of Pennsylvania. As chief executive of one of the largest states in the nation, he was—as in his life generally—unconventional and noncomplacent. Many viewed him as a refreshing change to politics as usual in the state capitol; others referred to him as a stubborn young governor who was unyielding on the principles in which he believed.

The Leader administration professionalized state government through expansion of Civil Service and merit selection, implemented the commonwealth's first significant Civil Rights legislation, created the Pennsylvania Industrial Development Authority to revitalize the economy, and reformed an overcrowded and treatment-deficient state hospital system. He signed the commonwealth's first law to provide education to children with disabilities. In the era of Sputnik and the Cold War, Governor Leader placed a high value on education and expanded aid to state-owned colleges that would ultimately become the State System of Higher Education. His administration also implemented novel laws to reclaim strip-mines that scarred the commonwealth's landscape, set out to establish a world-class state park system, and broke ground for the nation's first state-run vocational rehabilitation center at Johnstown, Cambria County.

There were failures, too. His plan to implement a graduated income tax failed miserably. Governor Leader was forced to sign a sales tax increase from 1 to 3 percent to deal with a budget deficit. His plan to take his skills to the U.S. Senate upon completing the governorship in 1958 came up short, too. Philadelphian Hugh Scott and the Republican political machine proved too strong a match. And his plans to run for governor again in the 1960s never materialized.

George Leader is diverse, complex, and maverick-like in his talents, skills, and interests, yet unpretentious in his values. He is an extraordinary multitasker even as he approaches a century of life. In addition, he was not only a pioneer in Pennsylvania politics: Following his term as governor, Leader turned his talents to mortgage banking and, soon after, to the nascent long-term care industry. With the assistance of his family he founded Leader Nursing and Rehabilitation Centers that garnered a groundbreaking reputation for quality care and compassion for Pennsylvania's aging population. He sold that company in 1981 and then founded County Meadows Retirement Community. At the time of his retirement as chief executive officer at 80 years old (1998), Country Meadows had ten campuses across the commonwealth with 3,200 residents. Following retirement from Country Meadows, Governor Leader established Providence Place Retirement Communities with four locations in Pennsylvania and a resident capacity of nearly 700 by 2010.

Leader has remained active in public affairs, serving as a delegate to Democratic National Conventions, supporting various candidates for public office, and weighing in on political and public policy issues. As a humanitarian his philanthropy extends to organizations such as Second Chance Ministries, which serves inmates in the commonwealth's correctional system, the Harrisburg School District in an effort to encourage students to pursue college as a career, international organizations such as C.A.R.E., and a Christian mission program in Ghana. The government of Israel named a reforested area near Jerusalem Leader Woodlands in honor of his philanthropy and public mindedness. The Harrisburg Area Community College awarded him an honorary degree. He holds several honorary degrees.

George Leader resides near Hershey. Mary Jane, his wife of over 70 years, passed away in the spring of 2011. They are the parents of three sons Michael, David, and the late Frederick Leader, and a daughter, Jane Janeczek. They have eleven grandchildren and one great-grandchild. An advocate for and living example of wellness in mind, body, and spirit, Governor Leader authored two books entitled *Healing Poems. Pennsylvania Heritage,* the commonwealth's leading history publication, has called him "Pennsylvania's Leader." Throughout his remarkable life, Governor Leader has earned the respect and admiration of people from all walks of life.

I first encountered Governor Leader when he delivered the commencement address to my graduating class at College Misericordia (now a university) in May of 1984. I knew who he was because my parents would refer to public servants like him in the same vein as Presidents Roosevelt and Kennedy. Yet, I had never heard him speak and was moved by what he told us graduates about service to others, giving back what we had been given, and simple human kindness and generosity. I was a history major graduating Magna Cum Laude and was very proud that day. Governor Leader reminded the graduates to remain both humble and grateful. At that time I realized that I wanted to one day get to know him better.

In 1987 I began working for the newly elected administration of Governor Robert P. Casey (1987–1995) in Harrisburg. One of the initiatives for which I later became responsible was the Children's Health Insurance Program (CHIP) signed into law by Governor Casey in 1992. My first personal encounter with Governor Leader occurred one day in the fall of that year when he called the governor's office to find out who was responsible for CHIP. He was referred to me and I took the call. He raised his voice, vehement that CHIP should be enrolling more eligible children and annoyed that former Philadelphia Eagles coach Dick Vermeil was on TV promoting CHIP, thinking that Vermeil was being paid from funding that should have been used to insure children. I assured him that we were doing all we could to enroll more children and that Mr. Vermeil was not being paid from CHIP funds but instead through Independence Blue Cross, an organization of which Governor Leader was not too terribly fond as he felt they charged customers too much and had excessive profits in spite of being a nonprofit, legislatively established health insurer.

He was satisfied; I was not. I wanted to know more about him. We soon met over lunch and got to know one another on a personal level. I found a lot in common with him, in particular the gift of curiosity and the ability to hold an informed discussion about many diverse issues. When I started working as a historian for the Pennsylvania Historical and Museum Commission in 1997 I knew that I wanted to write about Governor Leader to share his remarkable story with the public. I was especially intrigued by three things about him. First, in its history Pennsylvania has had few governors that have come from such humble agrarian roots. Second, with the exception of Gifford Pinchot (1923–1927 and 1931–1935) no other governors have been quite as progressive with the possible exception of Milton Shapp (1971–1979). Third, Governor Leader reaches back to a nearly forgotten era in state and local politics; by the end of the twentieth century, few people remained who could tell their story. In 2001, he agreed to provide several oral history interviews with me that resulted in an article in *Pennsylvania Heritage*.[1]

From that point forward, we continued our relationship, meeting frequently over lunch at Bob Evans in Hershey—his favorite restaurant—to talk about various topics. I got to know his wife, Mary Jane, and their children, all charming, gracious, and kind human beings. I introduced my family to Governor Leader and Mary Jane, and she even agreed to serve as pen pal to my daughter Abby for a fifth-grade school project. When my family was faced with serious illness Governor Leader always had words of encouragement, and he introduced me to Greg Anderson, cancer survivor, author, and founder of the Cancer Recovery Foundation of America. Greg's literature and words offered hope. Governor Leader continued to provide helpful literature and kept in touch. I thanked him for his concern but he insisted that saying thank you was not necessary. I knew it was simply his way.

In late 2008, Governor Leader asked if I would consider working with him on his biography. I did not have to think too much about it. We met for a series of oral history interviews in the spring and summer of 2009. I also interviewed his brother Henry, his children, and Mary Jane. With the assistance of my son, Aaron, I organized his archives located at the Leader Library at Providence Place in Dover, York County. Upon its opening in 2010 the Leader Library is the only such institution of, by, and for a former Pennsylvania governor. Always one to provide levity, Governor Leader told me that Bill Clinton's library cost $75 million. His cost about $75,000. He thinks his is probably better!

From scouring his papers, photo albums, scrapbooks, and other items at Providence Place in Dover, York County, as well as the George M. Leader Papers at the State Archives of Pennsylvania, I learned even more about him. The oral history interviews were central to his history (I deposited copies of the oral history interviews for this book at the Leader Library and Pennsylvania State Archives for future researchers and scholars).

As a result of this research this is Governor Leader's biography. Much of the text is written in his own words and those of his family, supplemented by primary and secondary sources. It is, however, more than a musing on one's life. At the same time it is a reflection on Pennsylvania politics and history during the twentieth century from the viewpoint of someone who lived the history, was shaped by it, and actually *made* some of it as well. This biography also stands as the most comprehensive published oral history account offered by any Pennsylvania governor since the commonwealth's founding in 1681.

I have tried to keep my personal interpretations to a minimum. In my work as a historian I have found it to be more effective to provide only the historical context and let the storyteller speak. This biography draws upon Governor Leader's life experiences as *he* tells about them. Here the reader can learn the story of how a human being from humble beginnings remained generous, humble, and kind, experienced successes and failures, tried his best to not forget where he came from, and remained passionate about issues that impact those who are sometimes dismissed and forgotten by society.

On occasion we meet people on the path of life that leave a lasting impression on us. When I first encountered George Leader in 1984 intuition told me he was one of those people. My hunch was correct and many others that know him had already figured that out. After spending many hours in his company I've concluded that he is among the most interesting people that I have ever met and he certainly ranks high on the list of Pennsylvania's most influential people of the twentieth century.

Here is his story as he largely tells it.

Note

1. Kenneth C. Wolensky, "Born a Leader for Pennsylvania," *Pennsylvania Heritage* XXVIII, no. 1. Winter, 2002. 22-29. Taped interviews were conducted on the following dates: June 15, 2001; October 18, 2001 with Governor and Mary Jane Leader; November 26, 2001; and, with Henry Leader, Governor Leader's brother, on November 15, 2001. Copies of these interviews are on deposit at the George M. Leader Family Archives, Providence Place, Dover, York County. In some instances these interviews are utilized here to supplement oral histories conducted in 2009.

1

Early Years, Parents, and Family

A Brief History of York County and the Leader Family

York County was created on August 19, 1749, from part of Lancaster County. Scholars attribute its naming to the Duke of York, an early patron of the Penn family, as well as York in England. Its county seat is the City of York. York County is located in the Susquehanna River valley, a large fertile agricultural region in South Central Pennsylvania.

Farming has guided Pennsylvania's economic growth and cultural development and has profoundly shaped the lands and people of the commonwealth throughout its history. South Central Pennsylvania, including York and its environs, was desired by white settlers for its rich agricultural lands. Prior to white European settlement, archaeological evidence has demonstrated that Native Americans were planters for thousands of years especially in the fertile river valleys. As early as 1682, William Penn and his heirs negotiated with the Indians to formally purchase land chiefly east of the Appalachians. As European settlements along the East Coast grew in size and number, the need for westward expansion became apparent, and in 1722, early white settlers of Penn's Woods secured agreement from Indian tribes to go inland. A tract measuring 6 miles wide and 15 miles long became the City of York and was surveyed and named Springettsbury Manor for Springett Penn, the grandson of the founder. The Onondaga, Seneca, Oneida, and Tuscarora nations signed a treaty of peace and deeded to the Penns "all the river Susquehanna and all land lying on the west side of said river to the setting of the sun."[1] Meanwhile, in 1729, John and James Hendricks had made the first authorized settlement in what is now York County, on Kruetz Creek. Germans, originally lured from the Rhenish Palatinate by William Penn's agents, soon followed Englishmen into the new frontier. Pamphlets and even playing cards extolled the opportunities to be found in Pennsylvania. Early Irish and Scottish settlers occupied land in the southeast, then known as York Barrens. To the north, Quakers moving from Chester County settled Newberry Township and its surroundings called the Redlands.

The town of York was laid out in 1741 when Thomas Cookson surveyed 437.5 acres on the banks of the Codorus Creek. On November 23, 1741, applicants agreed to pay seven shillings a year for the use of lots measuring 230 feet long and 65 feet wide and to erect on it "a substantial dwelling of 16 feet square at least . . . within the space of one year."[2] On August 17, 1749, the Provincial Assembly separated York County from Lancaster County and officially partitioned the new county. Hanover, at the time the second largest town in the county, was a thickly grown grove of hickory trees until 1763 when Richard McAlister laid out a town in what was referred to as a no-man's land that was claimed by Maryland as well as Pennsylvania. The border between the two provinces had been hotly contested. The rivalry became so bitter that the British government arranged a survey to settle the matter and a line was laid down by engineers Mason and Dixon in 1763–1767 eventually defining the Civil War geographic division between the North and the South.

As early as July 4, 1774, York Countians selected a committee to protest against British taxation and other oppressive measures. When Boston was blockaded as a result of its famous tea party, York County provided financial help and military support. A local company of militia were among the first from west of the Hudson River to march to Massachusetts. In 1775, there were 3,349 volunteer militiamen from the county. By 1778, a total of 4,621 people from York County answered the call to arms. The county's total population at the time was just shy of 25,000. In 1779 Colonel Thomas Hartley observed that "the York district has armed first in Pennsylvania and has furnished more men for the war and lost a greater number of men in it than any other district on the continent of the same number individuals."[3]

The presence of the Continental Congress in York from September 30, 1777, to June 27, 1778, brought the first printing press to the county. The press was necessary in order for military and legislative news to be sent throughout the colonies. It printed nearly $10 million in currency—money that was hyperinflated and quickly became worthless. The most important business conducted in York by Congress was the drafting of the Articles of Confederation that, in 1781, was ratified by the required two-thirds of the colonies. Full independence for the new nation followed in 1783.

It was around this time that the first known Leader (the name was recorded as Leider) lived in York County. Heinrich Leider and his two children (Anna Maria and Friedrich) were recorded in the register of Rev. John Waldschmidt, a Berks County pastor who had served several congregations.[4] Though very little is known about Heinrich, including with whom he fathered two children, at some point he migrated from Berks County—an important German immigrant destination—to Lancaster County (from which York County was created). Slightly more is known about his son Friedrich. Revolutionary War pension papers indicate that he was born in Lancaster County on January 31, 1760, and married Susanna Schreid, who was born on April 28, 1765. Friedrich died on April 29, 1844, and is buried in the Spry United Brethren Cemetery. During the Revolution, Friedrich served as a private assigned to a division of the Pennsylvania Regiment commanded by a Colonel Huber. Given his year of birth Friedrich could not have been older than his midteens when he took up arms. Friedrich engaged in skirmishes against Indians and British and he was attached to what was known as the wagon department, driving a team loaded with military stores. He was discharged on November 26, 1782, and granted a pension in 1833 (it was not uncommon for veterans of the Revolution to wait years for such a pension) that was passed to his wife following his passing. Friedrich and Susanna had twelve children: (in order of birth) Salome, Rebecca, Elisabeth, Susanna, Anna Mary, George, Johannes, Joseph, Catharine, Veronica, Charles (Carl), and Hanna. Large families were, of course, common at the time.

When Adams County was created from York County in 1780 the latter boasted a population of 25,643. By the Civil War, it had grown to 68,000, and the 1920 census recorded 144,000 people.[5] During the first half of the nineteenth century York remained primarily a rural and agricultural community but residents continued to contribute to the growing industrialization of the county. It was here that Friedrich and Susanna's son, George, appeared with the surname Leader, differing from his grandfather and father's spelling. He was born in Lower Chanceford Township on October 2, 1794, and died on December 27, 1878. He is interred at Salem Church Cemetery in present-day Jacobus, not far from Leader Heights. Here, many of the Leaders are at rest.

George married Eva Weiser on May 7, 1819, at Christ Lutheran Church in the City of York. As a young man George was a teacher in Springfield Township. According to Prowell's York County history: "He finally purchased the old homestead farm (of his parents) upon which he made many improvements, becoming one of the more prominent and influential citizens of the township and there continuing to be identified with agricultural pursuits until his death."[6] George and his wife had twelve children: Catharine, Charles, Susan, Priscilla, Sarah, George, Henry, Jesse, Elizabeth, Lydia, Elisa, and Anna Marie.

Next in the progression to the life of Governor Leader was the son of George and Eva, Henry Leader, who was born on December 27, 1830, and died February 5, 1916. He, too, is buried in Salem Cemetery along with his wife, Leah Wambaugh. They were married on January 8, 1854. Henry was a farmer and later in life moved to Codorus Township to purchase and operate a sawmill. Prowell noted that Henry, like his father, was a staunch Democrat and a devout Lutheran (his namesake and Governor Leader's brother, Henry, explains why the Leaders were Democrats in chapter 6). Henry and Leah had four children: Alice, George M., Priscilla, and Leah.

In the late nineteenth and early twentieth centuries, the county industrialized as did most of the northeastern United States. In his book, *Made in York*, historian Georg Sheets has documented the numerous products that were manufactured in the county during this era, including automobile bodies, ceramics, pottery, dinnerware, engines, hosiery, ice cream, fur coats, flooring, furniture, glass products, liquor and beer, typewriters, and pretzels. Numerous farming implements and machinery were also manufactured.[7] As was true throughout the county's history, entrepreneurship and invention were common. In 1825, John Elgar launched America's first iron steamboat named the *Codorus* on the Susquehanna River. The York Imperial apple, a popular and nationally recognized version of the fruit, was a county creation and a hybrid from other types of the fruit. And, of course, the currency printing press was unique to York during Congress's stay there. In the twentieth century the commonwealth's first Pinchot Road—a program launched by Governor Gifford Pinchot to provide good roadways for farmers —was built in Rossville. In addition, the father of world weightlifting and founder of the York Barbell Club was a county resident. Bob Hoffman (1898–1985) was a U.S. Olympic weightlifting coach (1948–1964) and actively promoted the sports of power lifting and bodybuilding. He served as an official advisor on youth physical fitness for Presidents Eisenhower, Kennedy, and Nixon, and he founded the York Barbell Company on Broad Street in 1932.[8]

During this period of rapid industrialization and agricultural growth lived Governor Leader's grandfather and grandmother, George M. Leader and Susan Myers Leader. They, too, were devout Lutherans, and at 19 years old, George began working for his father and purchased a farm in Shrewsbury Township where he remained for three years. As Governor Leader's life attests, the Leaders are not usually ones to stay put. Such was the case with his grandfather. In the late 1880s he moved to Glen Rock and became associated with Glen Rock Manufacturing Company whose products included doors, sashes, blinds, and other household and construction items. In 1899 he purchased another farm in York Township that, according to Prowell, was quite substantial. While he was apparently interested in public affairs, George never held public office but was a member of the county Board of Health. George appeared to be nonpartisan and supported office seekers and holders based on judgment and character. While it is not possible to know for sure it would be unlikely that he deviated too much from his father's political leanings as it was very common during this era for middle-class sons to follow their fathers not only in business affairs but also in civic matters and political ideology as well. George and Susan had one child, Guy Alvin, born October 21, 1887 (he died in 1978).

As the county continued to expand its population, agriculture, and industry Guy grew into a young man with quite a respectable reputation. He attended and graduated from York Collegiate Institute and taught in area public schools for nearly ten years. He also served as a school board director and began a career as a poultry farmer in 1911 as the Progressive Era took hold on the American political and social milieu. He and his wife, Beulah Boyer (1889–1967), were married in 1908 and were active members of St. Paul's Lutheran Church. By the end of the "roaring twenties" Guy was very prominent as a poultry man and earned the title of master farmer by the Pennsylvania Farmers Association in the early 1940s. He filled out the term of State Senator Lanius who had died in 1943 and was elected to the post in 1948. As Governor Leader later explains, his mother was not only central to managing the household and children but she also knew the importance of saving and worked extremely hard. Guy was the mover, the innovator, and always had new ideas. Both mother and father undoubtedly passed on important values to each of their seven children: Paul, Guy Jr., Lois, George, Henry, Mary, and Jean.

By the time Guy Leader launched his poultry business, agriculture was, by far, the county's dominant industry. From the end of the Civil War to the early-to-mid-twentieth century, farmers committed their plots of land to growing sorghum, corn, wheat, rye, barley, and other cash crops. Livestock farming was prominent and included cattle, chickens, and pigs. It was common for cash crop farmers, including the Leaders, to take their goods to downtown York's market every week in the summer and fall. Such farmers earned the moniker "truck farmer" as they used trucks and wagons to transport items to and from the city. Indeed, by 1940, Governor Leader's father was recognized not only as an important poultry farmer but as one who innovated with new techniques such as contour farming that mitigated soil erosion and conserved rainwater. Guy reported to the *York Daily Record* that the farming method enabled his birds to range on the grass strips between rows of corn, enjoy their shade, and cause no crop damage. His chickens were fatter and healthier.[9] It boded well for the political careers of Guy and George Leader that the family grew only legitimate crops and livestock. The York Police reported that illegal growing of marijuana, though not widespread, had raised concerns especially among the county's Christian population and had resulted in numerous arrests. The problem was new to the commonwealth, and some users reported that they enjoyed marijuana because it stimulated uncontrollable laughter, feelings of happiness, dreaminess, and "rapid flow of sexual ideas."[10] The Leaders likely were not very happy about the marijuana problem.

The county's annual agricultural and industrial exhibition, the York Fair, drew thousands of people by the early twentieth century. Such fairs were held in numerous Pennsylvania counties and served as a model for the creation of the Pennsylvania Farm Show in 1917. The year George Leader was born, 1918, the fair had to be canceled due to the Spanish flu epidemic. In the fall of that year the York Hospital was so overwhelmed with patients that the staff was required to use the fairgrounds as a treatment facility. In fact, so many people had died in York County from the flu that morticians reported to be running out of caskets.[11]

From the 1920s through the 1940s more than half of the county's nearly 150,000 people lived in rural areas and were engaged in some aspect of agriculture. Within the 903 square miles of the county, in 1940 there were 7,000 farms averaging 62 acres that were overwhelmingly farmed by their owners and occasionally leased. The county ranked an impressive third nationally in the value of its poultry products, had raised more turkeys than any other county in the eastern United States, produced 17 million eggs valued at nearly $5 million, and had 1.7 million hens. The Guy A. Leader Poultry Breeding Farm was certainly a principal contributor to the growing business of poultry farming and was ranked among York County's most productive of such farms.[12] The Leaders were recognized as influential in the poultry industry and produced over one million leghorn baby chicks each year that were sold to poultry farmers in Pennsylvania, Maryland, and New Jersey.

Governor Leader's Memories of Youth in York County

Common expressions about history are that life was simpler back then, less hectic, and family was important. Depending on one's own experience and interpretations, such assertions may or may not be true. By most accounts it is quite evident that hard work was common when it came to farming. It was into this environment of agriculture, burgeoning industry, the First World War, the Spanish flu epidemic, Woodrow Wilson as president, and, perhaps, simplicity and hard work that George M. Leader was born in January of 1918. Governor Leader explains:

> KW: Governor, what is your earliest memory?
>
> GL:[13] I have a photograph of my sister Mary and my brother Paul—Mary was eight years older than I was, and Paul was five years older—and myself taken in a studio in York, Pennsylvania. That photograph shows me with very short bobbed hair and my sister Mary with a big bow in her hair. I remember that photograph being taken. Beyond that, when I was a very small child—and I'm not sure that I remember this or that I was reminded of it by my mother—when I was about ten months old I seem to have been speaking in sentences—not very many sentences—but my mother drew a pencil sketch of what we call "the duck." I could say—go to my mother with a piece of paper—and say, "Mother, make a duck." Didn't say, "Draw a duck," I said, "Make a duck." She would draw for me. I found great satisfaction in that, but don't ask me why because we were in the chicken business, and we didn't have a single duck on the farm.
>
> KW: Your name—Leader—what's the German derivation of it?
>
> GL: If you go back, originally it was Lüder. My ancestors were illiterate when they came here. At some point later on, probably when they started going to the public schools, well some schoolteacher said, "What's your name, sonny?" and one of them said, "Leider." Or he saw the name written with the umlaut; he said part of the "u" has got to be an "I," so I'll just put an "e." So for a long time, our name was Leider in English. Several generations ago it started being Leader. And I think some schoolteacher just spelled it phonetically. It's hard for us to realize what kind of a world it was before there was literacy.
>
> KW: What would have been the German pronunciation?
>
> GL: "Lüder." The "u" would be slurred. I don't know what "luder" means, but "leider" means singer, and "lieder" would be leather. And I asked a German person one time what the umlaut means. He said, "You don't want to know. It's a bad word." So, I haven't further investigated it; I was discouraged.
>
> KW: Your first name, George, was passed down from where?

GL: My grandfather was named for his two grandfathers, George Leader and Michael Wambaugh. And in the cemetery at the Salem Church in Jacobus there are several George Leaders. Some of the tombstones were starting to fall over, so I went to a tombstone man and I said, "Why are they falling over?" And he said, "Because they used steel, iron pins between the base and the tombstone itself." And I said, "Well, what can we do about it?" And he said, "Well, I can put a base in for you and we can use bronze pins." I had the tombstones righted for the Leaders at Salem Union Cemetery at Jacobus. Three or four percent of the burials are Leaders including my mother and father. I purchased lots for myself, children, and grandchildren. I've already put the tombstone on my grave; figured maybe my children wouldn't get around to it! Really, though, I just felt I wanted to be sure it was put there and had it all set up with my own name and my wife's name on the front of the stone and my four children's names on the base. I said to the man from whom I bought it, "Can I put something on the back of that tombstone?" It's a pretty good sized tombstone. And he said, "Sure. What do you want to put on it?" I said, "I would like to put on the back of the tombstone: 'The essence of life is nonjudgmental, unconditional love.'" So I'll be preaching after I'm dead!

KW: Tell me about your mother and father.

GL: My mother was a remarkable person in many ways. She grew up on a general farm in York County. In those days it had maybe ten or twelve cows which had to be milked twice a day. They also grew some tobacco, corn, wheat, oats, and hay. Of course, all the power was horse power—they had horses. Most of the farmers in that area had two or three horses, or two or three mules. Some had more. My mother started school, and they spoke Pennsylvania Dutch at home. She started to understand and master English when she went to school. So she had to milk cows in the morning, then she went to school and came home after school and had to milk the cows again and help her mother with supper. After supper she and her father would go out to the tobacco shed and strip tobacco. Stripping tobacco means simply pulling the leaves off the stems. After it is hung in the tobacco shed long enough the leaves become dry and then it is graded by size and sold to brokers who trade in tobacco. My mother had the equivalent of a fifth-grade education. I remember she read the newspaper—the local paper—every day. When she and dad would go on vacation, which wasn't very often, she would write a letter and her penmanship wasn't bad. She had a very legible writing and a clear mind. Mother grew up in that atmosphere. I know when my oldest sister was ready to go to college she went to West Chester State College. My mother didn't think it was necessary to educate a girl but my father was a strong advocate of education. He brought us up to believe that we were going to go to college and all of us did except my brother Paul. He dropped out of high school his junior year, and my father helped him buy a farm, and he became a turkey breeder. Paul was very successful. He also had the good fortune of marrying a girl who inherited about $2 million. I said maybe it was better to have the $2 million than go to college. Who knows? My mother understood only one kind of wealth: money in the bank. She understood that perfectly—the money in her pocketbook. She put up with my father who was always in debt. He'd borrow $800 to build two chicken houses. He'd pay that off and he'd borrow another $800 to build two more until they had housing for 25,000 chickens. It was one of the biggest breeding farms in Pennsylvania.[14] My mother and father were quite different in terms of taking risks.

KW: Tell me about your father.

GL: My father—if he had the chance to go to college, which he didn't—he should have gone all the way to graduate school and become a college professor. He was a real scholar. He loved to read. He loved to study and he loved to share with us and his friends all this knowledge that he acquired. He read every night from about 6:30 to 9:30. I think he got almost all the magazines that were readily available. He purchased them from Curtis Publishing: *Colliers, The Saturday Evening Post, The American Magazine, The Ladies Home Journal*. He received all of the farm magazines: the *Pennsylvania Farmer, Maryland Farmer, The Poultry Tribune*. He got political magazines: *The Nation* and *The New Republic*. He got religious magazines—we were Lutheran—he got *The Lutheran* and *The Christian Century*. He also read two newspapers. He read the local paper, and whenever he got into the city—three or four times a week—he would pick up a copy of the *Philadelphia Record*, which was the liberal newspaper out of Philadelphia. Dad was the one who led the table conversation, and we talked about government. Dad ran for school board a couple times. He was elected once or twice. He served as state senator from York County in the 1940s and ran for Congress in 1948, but then withdrew. He was interested in state government and we were always very familiar with what was going on in Harrisburg. He was interested in the federal government and we followed the Roosevelt administration particularly. Everybody either loved Roosevelt or hated him and our family loved him. I think it was the love for Roosevelt that really motivated me to want to get more deeply involved in politics.

KW: You mentioned that your father talked about voting for Williams Jennings Bryan.

GL: He walked into the courthouse in York to hear the election returns in the William Jennings Bryan and William Howard Taft election of 1908. As he was walking home after Bryan lost the election, he said, "The only consolation I have is that I still have my girlfriend"—my mother, Beulah Naomi Boyer. He was heartbroken over Bryan. Later in life, I gave him a photograph—a big picture of Williams Jennings Bryan. And when he died, that was part of my inheritance. Dad was a liberal, and Williams Jennings Bryan could be considered in today's world a right-wing fundamentalist. In the Scopes Monkey Trial, he took the fundamentalist position, but in most matters he was very liberal. Many of the ideas for the New Deal of the 1930s may well have originated with Bryan. My father was not a fundamentalist. He was more liberal in his thinking.

KW: Your dad was a schoolteacher.

GL: Yes, he started as a schoolteacher. He got into it by accident. One of the stories he recalled was that when he taught he had to walk about a mile and half to fire up the furnace in his country school at six o'clock in the morning. The students arrived at eight o'clock and the building would be warm by the time they got there in the winter. He suffered from poor health, couldn't walk very well at all and he had a bad heart. That's one of the reasons why he couldn't continue to teach—because of his rheumatic fever. He had his teeth and tonsils removed. Then he began to recover. It was during that period, when he was really more or less flat on his back, that he said, "I'm not going to try to do ten men's work; I'm going to try to learn to supervise ten men." That was the real leap in his approach as to how he was going to lead his life. Most times, when I was growing up, he had fifteen or twenty men working for him in the poultry business. He treated them all very well. This was in the day when most people lived in houses without bathrooms, modern kitchens, or modern conveniences.

All of his employee houses had modern kitchens and bathrooms. When one of my father's employee's wives wanted wallpaper in a room, she got the wallpaper because my father said, "If you can keep the wives happy, you can keep the men happy." He had someone cut the lawn on all those properties once a week and kept them all trimmed up and looking nice. Those wives were happy!

KW: You were one of how many children?

GL: Well there were seven of us. I had three brothers and three sisters. My sister Mary was eight years older than I was—Mary Elizabeth. And my brother Paul was five years older than I—Paul Henry Leader. Then myself. My next brother after me was Guy Alvin Leader Jr. and then next one after that was Henry Boyer Leader, named for my Grandfather Boyer, who was a wonderful man. And the next one after that—a couple of years after that—was Margaret Jean Leader, and the next one after that was Ruth Lois Leader. That was the seven of us. My father always told us that even though we were really modern farmers with a very moderate income, we were all going to go to college. All of us did except my brother Paul.

KW: Why were the Leaders prominent in the community?

GL: Well my grandfather, for whom I was named and for whom Leader Heights was named, was on the school board for many years. I can remember there were quite a few times that he was elected president of the school board. It rotated, but he had his turns as president of the school board, running those 17 schools. My father believed in public schools and, as I said, he was a teacher and later served on the school board, too. York County, in those days, was more Democratic than Republican. Our township tended to be Democratic. The Leaders were Democrats; I came from a liberal democratic family that worshipped Roosevelt. We thought the Holy Trinity was God, Jesus, and Franklin Delano Roosevelt. One of the things about Roosevelt that I admired was that he was willing to try anything that might succeed and he was willing to risk failure.

We had a blind state senator in York County, Senator Lanius, a wonderful man. He died in the first or second year of his third term. This was the mid-1940s. He had been a school director for a couple of terms and worked very hard to do anything to consolidate and have modern schools. Most of the other board members were against it. He couldn't accomplish much in York Township because of the school directors. The mood at York Township was very conservative and they didn't have the progressive ideas that he had in education. They were conservative Democrats or Republicans. They didn't want taxes to go up. My father was noticeable in politics because he was considered a leader in York Township. That got him elected (to a full term) as state senator in the same year that Harry Truman carried York County by 2,500.

KW: What were your work experiences through your teen years?

GL: My family was an organization that had to produce. We produced food in the garden and helped with packing eggs, gathering eggs, feeding chickens, doing whatever had to be done on the farm. I know there were children in our schools that came from dairy farms. You could smell it. They were working with the dairy cows because the odor of the cows was still on their clothing. So, hard work was common, even among children. I learned the work ethic from my mother because she did nothing but work about six and a half days per week. She took about two hours off on Sunday morning to go to church. We had some pretty good preachers in our church, as we went to the Lutheran Church in York where we had a series of excellent preachers, excellent ministers. Then she would come home from church and cook a big dinner. We would have a nice supper.

KW: What was it like being a teenager during the Great Depression?

GL: Well, we were growing up in the 30s and those were Depression years. Our state government was very careful about spending money. Gifford Pinchot was elected governor in a second term in the early 1930s (1931–1935), and he got the farmers out of the mud. The commonwealth took over 6,000 miles of township roads, rural dirt roads—which were fairly poorly maintained in many cases—and paved them. One of the Roosevelt programs, it was either Works Progress Administration or the Public Works Administration, made money available to the state for paving roads. They were interested in putting people back to work, even as we are now in 2009. Some of the stones (for roads) were even cracked by hand. They paved those 6,000 miles. We still have a lot of public roads in Pennsylvania. I think we have more state roads than all of the New York and New England states put together. That was thanks to Gifford Pinchot who was a very good governor. Another big issue in those days was the elimination of the Volstead Act that launched prohibition. Pinchot was a dry. He was very antialcohol and against legalizing alcoholic beverages. My parents were very antialcohol as Democrats, and so they liked Pinchot, a Republican, and voted for him.

We lived in a vegetable growing area, and people had small farms and grew vegetables. There were three farm markets in York: Eastern, Central, and City. Almost everybody in our community would go to market one or two days a week. Mostly two days a week: Wednesday and Saturday. Things were very inexpensive. I remember in the summer, if we weren't busy, we'd help our next-door neighbor to pick berries. We picked berries, strawberries, blackberries, raspberries, and currants and things like that for 2 cents a box. Now our neighbor got 10 cents a box for those berries. Two cents was pretty good. I remember I had all of $67 when I got married, and it was all my pigeon money, my dandelion money, and my berry-picking money. It sounds silly now to even think about having a savings account with $67, but back in the Depression, for kids, that was pretty good. It was the only money I ever earned. People say, "Did your father pay you to gather eggs, pack eggs, mow the lawn?" I said, "You've got to be kidding." The biggest money I ever saw was when we had our Sunday school picnic. My father would give me 15 cents, and the big problem I had was whether I should buy two ice cream cones at a nickel apiece and one bottle of soda, or shall I buy two bottles of soda at a nickel apiece and one ice cream cone for a nickel? That was the big problem! Most everyone had enough to eat because they had all those vegetables. They had a little flock of chickens and most everybody had a pig or two. We didn't need garbage collectors; we had pigs and chickens. They would eat anything. So they butchered once a year and sometimes they might have a young steer that they slaughtered, or they might buy a quarter of beef and process that beef at the same time they slaughtered one or two of the pigs. So they had that, they had eggs, they had chicken. Everybody had enough to eat. Some of them may not have had very good clothing, but they had clothing that was good enough to wear to school. Those that had big mortgages on their farms tended to lose them during the Depression, but the farms around us were mostly already paid for. They had very old automobiles or very cheap automobiles. But you didn't know that people were poor or that they suffered. Everybody was about the same. I remember that there was one mansion in the area. The

Bon Ton stores are a pretty big chain today and this is their third generation now. But I remember the Bon Ton was owned by the Grumbachers. They had an estate about a mile from us. And I remember that there was a huge silver beech tree in their yard. We used to sneak in and stand under that beech tree and just look at that house—just marvel at it—thinking "What do people do with such big houses?" I went there on my bicycle. I must have been about twelve. It was impressionable to a farm boy of modest means. We marveled at that, but the rest of us were all about the same. Everybody had enough to eat and there was no malnutrition that I knew of in our area. Also, in my early years as a teen when I was going to St. Luke's Lutheran Church, the minister had a son about my age, and he started a young people's group there called the Loyal Legion. The Loyal Legion, of course, had both girls and boys in their teens. And it was a wonderful group. It was sort of a leadership-training group. The same minister that started that program sent some of us to Camp Nawakwa, which was a leadership-training camp in Biglerville, Pennsylvania. I think I got a lot of benefit out of that, because as a country boy, to mingle with the young people from all over the area was broadening.

KW: You attended a very small country school from grades one through five. What are your memories of being in that small country school?

GL: It was the Ness Country School. I went there for grade one through eight five. That area is a big interchange now called Leader Heights on Interstate 83, just south of York. They destroyed the school, of course, to build the big interchange. My country schoolteacher's name was Harry Hildebrand. Harry was not a very cultured or educated man. He used the word "ain't" in class frequently. He wasn't a disciplinarian, and the students more or less ran the school and the teachers. I remember we had a pot-bellied stove that burned coal and we had to go for water. There was no well on those properties. With a buddy we would go for water. We volunteered to go for water whenever we could get away with it. We'd go to the nearest farm with small buckets and fill them about two-thirds full. Of course we'd be gone longer than we should have been! Then we'd come back and emptied the water into a common-property tank with a little spigot on it. Each student had his own cup. We didn't have paper cups, we had collapsible cups. There was another school about a mile and a quarter away. That schoolteacher was a disciplinarian. His name was Harry Hovis. He knew his mathematics and grammar. He was one fantastic teacher. Harry had a paddle over on the window sill. He didn't do a lot of paddling. Just to keep us on our toes he'd paddle somebody about once a month. The paddle was flat, about a half-inch thick and six inches wide. He'd pull somebody over the desk and paddle him, and it would crack like a gun. He should have been a college teacher instead of a country schoolteacher. After the fifth grade my father transferred me to that school (Jessop's School). I went through sixth, seventh, and eighth grade in two years and graduated. I passed the eighth grade examination when I was 12 years old. When I finished eighth grade and I took that eighth-grade examination, I was the top student in the township.

KW: Did you ever get paddled?

GL: No, I didn't get paddled. I was one of his prize students! If he ever had to paddle me I would have gotten it even worse when I got home.

KW: You were the top student when you were in eighth grade. What did it mean to be the top student?

GL: It didn't mean a doggone thing. I didn't consider myself smart or anything. I was very enthusiastic at that time in my life. I loved education. I loved learning. I think I was a little aggressive in those days. But there was really no great opportunity to show off your skills. But I'm sure Harry Hovis knew that I was a smart kid and he kept me on the ball. He kept me focused. Then I went to the York City schools for ninth grade. It was a junior high school. Penn was the junior high school. Dr. Glatfelter was the principal. He was a sweet, wonderful human being. Of course, I'm prejudiced; my grandmother was a Glatfelter. He was a distant relative, although at the time I didn't know it. The spirit at Hanna Penn was fantastic. When I was in junior high school, one of the teachers put together a tour group to go to the World's Fair in Chicago. We went by train and slept in dormitories at the University of Chicago. We were chaperoned of course. It was a great experience to go to Chicago. It wasn't very expensive for a trip of that size. The World's Fair was quite an experience for me.

KW: What was the transition like, going from a small country school to schools in York City?

GL: First, sometimes we walked the whole distance but most of the times we walked about half that distance and got a ride for the other half. Now if it was a rainy day, we went to a store where my family bought their groceries, and we called home and said, "It's raining. Can you pick us up?" In about a half an hour or an hour they came and got us. When I went across the street to William Penn Senior High School it was 180-degrees different. There was an arrogance about the administration and an arrogance about the teachers. They were all that way. I called it an education factory. They had to turn out so many graduates and, by gosh, they were going to turn them out no matter what. My father, who was really very well-informed about education matters, decided that I had to take both Latin and German. And for two years, I was taking both Latin and German. I was miserable because I'm a very weak language student. I just don't have that skill. Maybe I would have gotten it when I was very young but by the time that I got to languages I had a very tough time. In my senior year I only had German which was bad enough. I was unhappy at that school. I finished at William Penn and didn't learn how to write too well and wasn't too good at languages. Then I went to York Collegiate Institute for one year. We had an English teacher by the name of Mr. Snyder. We had to write a one-page essay every day. He went to the trouble of correcting it. He corrected the grammar, he corrected the punctuation. We got one back and gave him another one. He was a very conscientious teacher. And by the end of the year, I sort of learned to write. And I would not have been able to do the essay-type examinations in college if I had not had that experience, because I did not know how to put my thoughts down in writing. I didn't have any experience with that in high school. Yet, I graduated when I was 16. Then we moved into a new house when I was 16. A nice new brick house with four bedrooms. Dad built that house and a two-car garage.

KW: You graduated twelfth grade when you were 16 years old. Wasn't that unusual?

GL: Yes, I was the youngest in my class. I was sixteen and driving a car. I drove into York in the morning and home in the evening. Most of the kids there came from pretty well-to-do families, and they had given scholarships to half a dozen or more athletes who played sports. I got a varsity letter in football, a varsity letter in baseball, and a JV letter in basketball. I was on the honor roll every time and earned the chemistry prize for being the number one chemistry student. It was a great year because I drove there in the morning, went to school all day, played sports until supper time, came home and had supper, and did my homework. That year set me up for college because I hadn't learned how to write.

KW: What was college life like for you?

GL: I went to Gettysburg College. That was a big step for a country boy. Remember, this was in a time when college was almost unheard of for working people and people from farm families. I still had this problem with languages and writing even in college. As I said, when I went to YCI and had an English teacher by the name of Snyder; he required us to write a one-page essay every day, five days a week. He took the trouble of reading and making corrections and suggestions. By the end of that year, he had developed me to the point where at least I was a passably good writer. Not a great writer, but enough to get by. I said if I had gone to college without Mr. Snyder's instructions on how to write, I wouldn't have had the least idea how to handle an essay-type examination. So, I have to thank Mr. Snyder and York Collegiate Institute for that. Well, in my freshman year in college, I did very well except in one course. One semester I got a B and the other semester I got a C in German. I was still struggling with languages. And I was really upset with my performance. I had done well in everything else. So I went to summer school. I had to take two years of German. I got the freshman year behind me. Instead of taking the second year of German in my sophomore year, I went to summer school. You can imagine how unhappy I was, having to sit there all day long, studying German. I was the only student in the class so you couldn't hope you weren't going to be called on—you already knew you were. You had to be the performer. The professor was the listener. And I went that summer, and I finished the course. And about halfway through I felt so shaky about my ability. I thought, "Wouldn't it be terrible if I gave up my summer for this, and then failed the course?" But luckily, the good Lord smiled on me, and I made a B in that course for the summer. Mary Jane was very upset with me that I went to summer school instead of being home and taking her out on dates on Saturday nights. It would have been a great sacrifice for both of us if I hadn't passed the course. So from that point on I was almost always on the dean's honor role because language was my shortcoming. I really struggled with languages. But, I remember that I got a B the very first semester and a C the second in languages, and that knocked me off the honor role. Summer school helped, however. I did have a hard time there initially. I started as a chemistry major. Turned out I decided to become a philosophy major because I liked the philosophy professor. He was one of the best teachers I ever had. As a result I had trouble meeting the requirements of almost any major, but I had a good bit of sociology, economics, and history, etc. I somehow found out the University of Pennsylvania had a program and that I could easily meet the requirements to become a social studies major. Gettysburg College did not have that program. You had to have about 18 hours of history, 12 hours of economics, 12 hours of sociology, and 12 hours of political science. I had no trouble putting that all together, and I graduated with a Bachelor of Science degree in education. I was in Penn's school of education and I really loved that. I transferred to Penn in my junior year. If I had stayed one more year I would have had my master's. I always regretted I didn't do that; however, a few years later, I went back and earned a master's degree in public administration. For much of my life I probably would have been very happy if I had stayed in education, but I always had this yearning to be in politics.

KW: That was a big move for a boy from a farm to go to Gettysburg and then Penn.

GL: Yes. We visited Penn. My father and my brother Henry and I visited the School of Education. I remember Dean Minnick immediately signed me up. Then he said to my father, "What's this young fellow going to do?" regarding my brother Henry. He said, "Well he's going to go college somewhere." Henry had just graduated high school. The Dean said he had the phone number for Swarthmore College and that would be a good school for Henry. We called Swarthmore and made an appointment for him immediately. I always said, "Henry, I got you admitted to Swarthmore College, and they gave you a scholarship right off for $700 a year." My father kept meticulous records; he had three of us in college. Frankly, I don't know where he got the money to pay for it, because he had—dad's income came in around $10,000, which was pretty good in those days. But with Henry at Swarthmore, Guy Jr. at Penn State, and me at Penn, we were all costing our father about $1,100 each per year. So he had the three of us in college for about $3,300 per year.

KW: What years were you at Penn?

GL: I graduated with the class of '39, so it was in 1938 and 1939.

KW: When did you first meet Mary Jane?

GL: My future wife went to St. Luke's Lutheran Church in York, and they had an organization for young people that were in high school called the Loyal Legion, and she was in that and so was I. That's when we first got acquainted. I probably met her when I was 14 or 15—in the early 1930s. We didn't pair off in those days, but everyone understood that Mary Jane and I were more attracted to each other. There were other girls in the Loyal Legion, and they were a bit conniving. Girls didn't ask boys for dates in those days, but they had other more subtle ways of working it out. The girls in that group were Mary Jane, Sarah Elizabeth Rouck, who married a Lutheran minister later, Ruth Zimmerman—her father was very prominent in the church there, and Bee Weickert. The boys were Joe Thompson, Bill Sprenkle, Fred Rudisill, the minister's son, and myself. The Loyal Legion was a very interesting young people's group—very well led.

We had a preacher who was a real scholar, Dr. Earl S. Rudisill. He had a son in our age group, Fred. I used to be a guest at their home for dinner. It was the first time I was anywhere that they had napkins on the table. Where I grew up you'd use your sleeve or a handkerchief because we didn't have napkins. We didn't even have paper napkins at the table; nobody did in those days. Napkins were for rich people. It was quite a strain on me to eat at that table and see the array of silver because, you know, who needs two forks? I never sat down with two forks, two knives, and two spoons on the table before. I mean, this is a complicated procedure for a country boy from York Township! I ate at the Rudisill home, and it was a great experience. The Rudisills were great, and Dr. Rudisill and Mrs. Rudisill really cared about young people. Well, Mary Jane decided that I was going to be her partner in the Loyal Legion, I think because she knew I was so shy. Of course, I wasn't bad looking either! I think of the girls in the group, I was probably attracted to her a little more. The other girls in the group were nice girls, too, and all of them got married and had successful lives, but not necessarily got married to the guys that were in the group. Out of the four boys and four girls, we were the only two that got married. By the time I was 16 or 17, Mary Jane and I had our first date at the swimming pool at Hershey Park. I joined a group called the "High Y Club" at the YMCA in York. The club met once a week in the YMCA, and they had an annual picnic at the end of school. All the boys—it was an all-boys club of course—were to bring our dates. And my first date was with Mary Jane at the High Y Club. And we came to Hershey, and we swam in the pool, which is no longer there. When I was first dating Mary Jane, my father wouldn't let me have the car every Saturday night. He said I was too young to get serious, so I could only have the car every other Saturday night. So it was an every two-week romance! Mary Jane and I went to the movies in York. It cost 35 cents for a ticket to the movies at the Strand or Rialto. They had pretty good pictures in those days, mostly romantic pictures. After that, we'd go out to an ice cream parlor, and you could get a plate of ice cream for a nickel or a dime. So most of the time when I took Mary Jane out, the total cost of the date was a dollar. But it was very romantic for me, being a country boy. In those days, I didn't talk very much. Mary Jane did most of the talking, and she was very forthcoming. And we established a nice relationship. We have been married for 70 years. After 70 years of marriage, I think she is starting to get bored with me! She says, "George, you keep repeating the same stories that I've heard a hundred times." If we are in the presence of people that haven't heard the stories, I say to her, "But Mary Jane, the story is new to them!" She rolls her eyes!

KW: You maintained your relationship with Mary Jane through your college years. Tell me about that.

GL: Yes. She was very angry that I went back to summer school at Gettysburg College because she thought we were going to have some nice dates all summer long. But I only came home about once every three weeks or so. I was studying hard; I thought I might fail German. Wouldn't it be terrible to sacrifice my whole summer to accomplish this—to achieve completion of my language requirement, and then fail it? I was reporting to the head of the German department at his home since I was the only summer student in the class. I had to be prepared. The professor was a nice old man, Dr. Grim. I passed with a B. That was a miracle! I didn't deserve a B. I didn't really deserve it—it was a miracle. He must have liked me. But Mary Jane was not happy at that time because we were getting pretty serious, and I was away for the summer. Mary Jane had a very unfortunate experience at that time because they lost their home. Her father was in the insurance business. He sold life, fire, and casualty insurance. Customers just stopped paying. The insurance salesmen were paid out of the insurance premiums. Life insurance practically dried up during the Depression. Selling was next to impossible because people were struggling to put food on the table. So she had a tough time during that period. She weathered it fairly well. It is hard for people today to realize how tough it was on families in those days. I think it influenced her, though. Being married to someone like me who is more of a risk taker, having gone through that, I think some of the things that I undertook might have stressed her because she'd gone through such tough times as an adolescent.

Mary Jane's family had to move. She had three brothers, and the four of them were living in an apartment. Her one brother was in college, and he was only home in the summer. Their house had plenty of bedrooms, but they lost it because they couldn't keep up with the payments on the mortgage. Mary Jane was able to get a job. You could hardly buy a job in those days. She got a job at the telephone company as an operator. They had a whole row of telephone operators in those days. She made $13.45 a week. I'm sure she gave about ten dollars of that to her mother to put some food on the table, and she gave some of it to her brother who had an athletic scholarship at Syracuse University. She sent him some money because he needed it. Mary Jane had a chance to get a scholarship to Syracuse, but she couldn't take it because she couldn't supplement her income, and they needed that $13.45 at home.

KW: She was working while you were going to Gettysburg?

GL: That's right. And her family was going through a rough time. She and her mother were very close, and I wanted to get married a little sooner, but Mary Jane felt her family needed to have her income. The telephone company thought if you got married, you were lucky enough to have one income—one member of the family employed—and you had to resign if you got married. That was the company policy.

KW: Women had to resign if they got married?

GL: Yes. So when we were married, she had to resign; that was the tradition. I don't remember when I gave her the proposal ring anymore, but basically we were engaged when I was an upperclassman at Penn. I wanted to get married in June, as soon as I got out of Penn. She wasn't quite as anxious.

KW: How did you complement each other early on?

GL: I don't think very many of us think about that when we were young, maybe we should. Maybe if we thought about that more today there wouldn't be so many divorces. But my father always said "opposites attract" and we were opposites. It was odd that we liked each other because she came from a conservative Republican family that hated Roosevelt. I came from a liberal Democratic family. We loved Roosevelt. You can't risk success without risking failure. I think Mary Jane, even though she may have disagreed about some of my undertakings, once the decision was made she supported me 100 percent, just as my mother supported my father. Maybe my father is right, maybe opposites do attract, because we were quite different. Now Mary Jane was a good scholar; she was a language scholar, she got the Latin prize. I was lucky to pass. And if people are good in languages fine, if they are good in math and sciences fine, but you can't necessarily be good in both. Mary Jane was a master of languages.

KW: When were you married?

GL: September 17, 1939. My father gave me $15 for the minister and the music. We were married at church by one of our former pastors. I gave the minister $10 and the organist $5. A $15 wedding! And then he gave us $50 to go on our honeymoon. We went to New York City for six days on $50. Today you can't get a cab or lunch for $50 in New York! We went to the New York's World Fair in 1939. I think it actually began in '38 but they repeated it for a second year. On our honeymoon we stayed in a tourist home. I remember it had an iron bed in it and not a very good mattress. But we had those three days at the fair. I bought the tickets at the university. They had a sale on tickets there for students. Then we saw a great Broadway show, something with the name . . . America was in the title. I've forgotten. American Story or something of that nature. Then we went to Radio City and they had an in-house television, a closed-circuit television. Mary Jane and I saw ourselves on television and I said to her, not thinking that Mary Jane was as sophisticated as I was then, "Someday they'll be piping that right into our homes." And within ten years, they were. We went to Radio City Music Hall and saw *A Chorus Line*. All that for $50! We left on Sunday to go to New York and came back on Saturday afternoon with very little money left in our pockets.

KW: Where did you live after being married?

GL: The first six months we lived with my family, my mother and father. My wife was sick for six months with asthma. She had very bad asthma. Then we rented a place from my brother, Paul. He had apartments. He had a nice brick house that he changed into two flats. We got the first floor flat. We rented the first floor flat for $16 a month and shared the bathroom with the people on the second floor. It was pretty good. Paul's house had a recreation room in the basement with a ping-pong table. We used to go there and have tournaments. There would be a lot of shouting, teasing. Those were happy years.

KW: Where did you work?

GL: I worked for my dad after I came out of Penn. Dad gave me $25 a week. Dad was not well. He had been stressed too long, I guess. He was having trouble digesting his food, and my mother said, "George, come home and help your father before he dies." She knew he wasn't well. My father reached the point that he wanted to have a lot less responsibility, a lot less stress in his life, so I came home. He had a male secretary. Back in those days, there were a lot of male secretaries. It was a good stepping-stone for a lot of young men. So I came home and my father had a two-man office: himself and a male secretary. He stopped coming to the office, so I started writing his personal letters. I got caught once. A former coach at Penn State was one of his customers, and he called me and he said, "I know Guy didn't write those letters because I can tell the difference." He was smart. When I married Mary Jane, my salary got up to $35, even though I didn't deserve it. But Dad liked Mary Jane, maybe more than me! Compared to what he was paying his other employees, I was being overpaid. We were selling something over a million baby chicks a year to over four or five hundred customers. We had good customer relationships. They would come in and would want to see our place, and I would show them around. We also had a very complex breeding program. We had 2,500 chickens in trap nest facilities. A trap nest was designed so that when a chicken goes in to lay an egg, it gets trapped. It has a wing band and a leg band. You record the numbers from the bands on a sheet then weigh the egg and put it on the sheet and keep records on them. If there was a family that had five or six or seven or eight sisters (females) who all produce well, those are the bloodlines that you wanted to use for breeding. We had lots and lots of records on those birds. In a couple of years,

I wanted to expand the business. I always said I had desire to go to the Carolinas, being young and ambitious. But, Dad didn't want to.

KW: Could it have been that your father was at a point in his life where he didn't want to take any more risks?

GL: It might have been a risk factor because for the first time in his life, about the time when I got back from college, he was out of debt. He was debt free. He had a nice income. He might have been making about $25,000 a year at that point instead of the $10,000 that he had made through the Depression because times were getting better.

KW: You were more of a risk taker.

GL: I wanted to go down South. I could have gone down there without risking *too* much, but it would have been a risk, yes. Transporting eggs and putting a hatchery into operation in the South would have been a risk. Who knows whether they'd want to buy our baby chicks in the South? At that time I didn't have a marketing study.

As World War II loomed on the horizon, George was obliged to serve his country. Life for him and Mary Jane was put on hold, as were the lives of tens of thousands of GIs and their families. After the war the Leaders substantially engaged their entrepreneurial talents as poultry farmers. George then began his foray into politics.

Notes

1. Pennsylvania Historical and Museum Commission, "State Historical Markers," http://www.phmc.state.pa.us; George Beyer, *State Guide to Historical Markers of Pennsylvania* (Harrisburg: Pennsylvania Historical and Museum Commission, 2000).
2. George R. Prowell, *History of York County Pennsylvania* (Chicago, IL: J. H. Beers and Company, 1907), 47.
3. Prowell, *History of York County Pennsylvania*, 47.
4. Charles Glatfelter, *A Short Sketch of the Lieder-Leader Family of York County* (unpublished paper, n.d.).
5. United States Census, 1860 and 1920.

6. Prowell, *History of York County Pennsylvania*, 813.

7. Georg Sheets, *Make in York* (York, PA: Agricultural and Industrial Museum of York County, 1991), 136.

8. Pennsylvania Historical and Museum Commission, "State Historical Markers."

9. James McClure, "Technique Sows Success," *Never to be Forgotten: A Year-by-Year Look at Your County's Past* (York, PA: York Daily Record, 1999), 6.

10. James McClure, "Law Targets Marijuana," *Never to be Forgotten: A Year-by-Year Look at Your County's Past* (York, PA: York Daily Record, 1999), 4.

11. McClure, "Law Targets Marijuana," 2.

12. Betty Peckham, *The Story of a Dynamic Community: York, Pennsylvania* (York: York Chamber of Commerce, n.d.), 63.

13. George M. Leader, interview by Kenneth C. Wolensky, January 31, 2009, and April 17, 2009, Hershey, PA.

14. "York County Gives State Two Master Farmers," *York Gazette and Daily*, August 2, 1929, 6.

2

World War II and Early Political Ventures

Pennsylvanians contributed a great deal to World War II. Over one and a quarter million residents, a large portion of the commonwealth's population of nearly seven million, served directly in various branches of the U.S. Armed Forces. One out of every seven members of the U.S. Armed Forces was a Pennsylvanian. Hundreds of thousands who did not serve in the military supported the war effort close to home through their work, skills, volunteerism, and patriotism.

The roster of Pennsylvanians who managed the war effort included Army General and Chief of Staff George C. Marshall of Uniontown; General Matthew Ridgway of western Pennsylvania, Commander of the 82nd Airborne Division; General Jacob. L. Devers of York, Commander of the Sixth Army Group; General Joseph T. McNarney of Emporium, Deputy Allied Commander in the Mediterranean; and General Carl Spaatz of Boyertown, Commander of the American Strategic Air Forces in Europe. The U.S. Navy also had its Pennsylvania-bred leaders, including Chief of Naval Operations Admiral Harold R. Stark of Wilkes-Barre, who was also appointed Commander of American naval forces in Europe; Admiral Richard S. Edwards of Philadelphia, Deputy Chief of Naval Operations; and Admiral Thomas C. Kinkaid of Philadelphia, Commander of the Seventh Fleet in the South Pacific. Besides military fame, some veterans went on to greater achievements, such as Indiana native and actor, Jimmy Stewart, who flew

20 combat missions during the war, rose to the rank of brigadier general in the Air Force, and, later in life, received the Presidential Medal of Freedom.[1]

Strategic military encampments, depots, and reservations dotted the Keystone State, totaling 40 in all, such as Fort Indiantown Gap in Lebanon County and Philadelphia's Frankford Arsenal and Quartermaster Depot. More Congressional Medals of Honor were awarded to Pennsylvanians than to citizens of any other state, and commonwealth residents ranked among the top purchasers of war bonds. Also throughout the war years, citizens continued to vote in large numbers to ensure that this fundamental right of democracy was exercised to its fullest extent, especially during difficult times. For example, as the potential for war loomed in 1940, Franklin Roosevelt secured over 2 million votes in the Keystone state while his opponent Wendell Willkie earned nearly 1.9 million. During the height of the war in 1944, Roosevelt came in again with 2 million Pennsylvania votes while Thomas E. Dewey secured 1.8 million. U.S. senatorial elections were equally as important to Pennsylvanians. In 1940, 2.1 million votes sent Democrat Joseph Guffey back to the Senate for a second term; Democrat Francis Myers was elected to the Senate for the first time in 1944 with 1.9 million ballots cast in his favor. Electoral turn-out was similarly high in the gubernatorial election of 1942 when Republican Edward Martin was victorious with 1.4 million votes, while his opponent F. Clair Ross earned about 1.1 million.[2]

The Keystone State's rich reserves of fossil fuels—coal, oil, and their by-products—were essential to victory. For example, in 1944 mineworkers produced 64 million tons of anthracite coal and over 144 million tons of bituminous coal. A large portion of the commonwealth's coal fueled the war effort. The Pittsburgh Grease Plant of Standard Oil, Inc. produced over five million pounds of "Eisenhower Grease" used in military vehicles, ships, planes, and other transports. Allegheny County's Dravo Corporation Shipyard and its 16,000 workers manufactured over 1,000 Navy landing ship tanks or LSTs, in addition to munitions, hardware, vehicles, and other supplies. Many of the workers lived in nearby Mooncrest, a community of planned industrial housing built by the federal government. Along the Delaware River in eastern Pennsylvania, the Sun Shipbuilding and Dry Dock Company was the largest shipyard in the world during the war, where 35,000 workers built and repaired nearly 2,000 ships at this single location. In central Pennsylvania, factory workers in Hershey produced a special version of the famed chocolate bar by the tens of thousands for military food rations.

Industrial giant Bethlehem Steel stands out for its many contributions to the allied cause. The company had seen its work slow during the Great Depression, but with Roosevelt's Lend-Lease program (initiated prior to U.S. entry into the conflict to assist Great Britain and other allies with equipment and supplies) and following the Japanese attack on Pearl Harbor, Bethlehem Steel became indispensable. Its mills in Bethlehem, Steelton, Johnstown, and elsewhere worked day and night constructing armor plate and ships, including the famed aircraft carrier Lexington and the battleship Massachusetts. Bethlehem Steel was the nation's largest maker of ordnance, shells, air systems for submarines, and armor plate and components for aircraft engines.[3]

Pioneering developments came out of the Keystone State. In Butler, the American Bantam Car Company developed the prototype for the Jeep and built nearly 3,000 during the war. Critical to saving lives of the sick and wounded was adequate medical care and medicine. By the early 1940s, G. Raymond Rettew of West Chester pioneered the mass production of penicillin, the world's first antibiotic. Working with Wyeth Laboratories, his laboratory—a converted car repair shop—produced and shipped more penicillin to the Allied forces than any other lab in the world.

When histories of wars are written, the human impact is often overshadowed by the stories of the winners and, sometimes, the losers as well as the aura of might and dominance. However, history can also demonstrate that the human impact of war is deep and wide. During the World War II era, we need only look at the Holocaust or Hiroshima and Nagasaki to measure the human impact of the conflict, to say nothing of the overall lives lost, areas destroyed, dollars spent, and mental anguish that resulted. As people in Western societies live longer now than at any other time in human history, the World War II generation may be the first American cohort to have the advantage of ample time to reflect on their contributions and sacrifices. The combination of reflective time and ample collection of oral histories bears out the significance of the World War II generation. There are countless stories of ordinary people, hundreds of thousands in number, who worked, fought, voted, sacrificed, and raised families. Many Pennsylvanians could discover a story in their family or community relating to that time in American history. Oral histories have been collected that document the important and patriotic contributions of many Pennsylvanians during World War II.[4]

Here, Governor Leader shares his story:

KW: What stands out when you reflect on your World War II service?

GL:[5] There have been a number of miracles in my life, and the first one is the fact that I came back from World War II. And you might say, "Well, why do you think that's a miracle when a lot of people came back?" Well, I was on an aircraft carrier. We were preparing for an invasion of Japan. We were getting ready to land—the fleet was getting ready to land 500,000 men or so in Japan in an effort to take Japan and, in a sense, liberate it. Well, I was on a carrier, and we had about five or six carriers in the middle of the fleet in the Pacific. They would have been the first target of the kamikazes. Kamikazes were planes whose pilots were on a suicide mission. It was reported that there were 2,500 kamikazes—planes and pilots trained and ready to counteract any invasion. The first thing they would have done is knock out our carriers. They fly so low over the water that, if we dropped our aircraft guns down a level to fire at them, we would hit our own ships. You can't believe how many ships there were in the fleet at that time, and when they brought the seventh fleet up, with the tank carriers and the troop carriers and all the supplemental stuff, you can't imagine that many ships off the coast of Japan. So first they would knock the carriers out. It would be like fighting the war and losing *all* of your airports, *all* of your landing strips. Without aircraft carriers, American planes would just fly around until they go into the water and are ditched because they couldn't land. They didn't have their landing fields anymore. I was on one of those carriers. The chance of my being killed was real good. U.S. forces would have been too busy fighting a war to come by and pick up a couple of guys off a carrier that happened to survive. When a carrier was hit, the black oil was all over the water, and most of the time, it catches fire. You can hardly swim in it because there are four or five inches of tar (oil) on the water, maybe on fire or smoking—suffocation.

I think that's the first miracle, that I came back. The fact that they dropped the atomic bombs and we didn't invade Japan and probably avoided 500,000 casualties, many of them would have been dead. I think that's a miracle. Certainly, I sometimes think—well, there's some guilt. I wonder how many women and children died in Japan so that I could live and people like me could live.

KW: How did you start out in the Navy?

GL: I heard that the Navy had a supply training program at Harvard. It started out with a full year of training, but by the time that I came along, they reduced it to four months. I thought it would be nice to have the Navy send me up to Harvard for four months and become a supply officer. I, of course, was drafted, but because I farmed with my father I probably could have been deferred indefinitely. I was about 23 or 24 years old. So I left the farm. Soon after completing the program at Harvard, I applied for commission in the Navy supply corps. Well, the wheels of government grind slowly.

Probably six months later I got the commission. I went from one job to another—could have stayed in Philadelphia where I was initially stationed for the full length of the war. I was in Philadelphia for about six months. I wanted to make more of a contribution, however. I learned more about the supply corps, and then I signed on to a carrier service unit. I was assigned to the *USS Randolph*, an aircraft carrier, CV-15, which was the biggest type of carrier that they had for World War II. The huge ones that came out later—I think that Franklin Roosevelt may have been the first one—were huge, but they never got into combat in World War II. They were under construction at that time.

Off of the coast of Japan, 150 to 250 miles out, our mission was to send in bombers—pinpoint bombing—on Japanese targets. We would bomb for two or three days, then go back out a couple hundred miles and get refueled and reammunitioned, and replace the planes that we had lost. We had about 100 planes on the carrier and we always lost some—the pilots, too.

KW: Why did you choose the Navy and not another branch of the military?

GL: I was intrigued by being at sea on an aircraft carrier. I was proud to be an officer. And, I think the whole idea of going up to Harvard for four months appealed to me. I also liked the idea of supply. In the military, everybody forgets how important supplying the troops can be. Something like upward of 10 percent of carrier staff was dedicated to supply, an important job.

KW: What was your job, specifically, in supply division?

GL: In supply I had all the ship's spare parts, including a propeller shaft that was about 50 feet long. They put the spare parts on the ships in those days to be sure that they were there when they needed them: engines, wing parts, gear, leather jackets, and so on. I had put together a parts catalog when I was in Philadelphia. That came in very handy on the ship.

KW: What was it like leaving your wife and children behind?

GL: Well, we didn't have any children at the time, but Mary Jane was pregnant when I left. She lived with her parents for the duration of her pregnancy. It was stressful for both of us being apart during that time, but we knew it was important to serve the country. It was very interesting to come back to a wife and a baby. I missed them terribly; it is very hard not to see your newborn child until he is 9 months old. But, that was common during wartime.

KW: What do you remember about the dropping of the atomic bombs?

GL: We got word: "Get out of there 350 miles and stay out until further notice." So the carrier moved out to sea 350 miles. We didn't know why. Maybe the admiral did. I don't know. Then, about the time the engines were slowed, we heard that they had dropped the atomic bombs on Nagasaki and Hiroshima. That was the end of pinpoint bombing, no more need for that.

KW: What did the ship do then?

GL: We were supposed to be part of the group that went in with *USS Missouri* to take the surrender. We were within 90 or 100 miles of the surrender point when we received reverse orders to go back to Baltimore for Navy Day. So we went back to Hawaii, took the gunnels off the sides of the ship because we couldn't get through the Panama Canal with those gunnels on the ship.

I have to say that the Navy was a great experience. I learned a great deal, but I didn't want to make a career out of it. One of the things about the Navy, besides all of the good things I learned, was that the Navy taught people to smoke, me included. You couldn't buy cigars on our ship unless you bought a box. So

I bought them by the box. I not only smoked cigars, but I also chewed the cigar butts; it was like chewing tobacco. This was long before anyone made the connection between tobacco and cancer. Anyway, I gave up that habit before long.

KW: The World War II generation has often been referred to as "the greatest generation." You were a part of that generation. Do you think the statement applies?

GL: Well, I think the greatest generation was the greatest for two reasons. The fatalities both in Europe and the Pacific were unbelievably high, and the people that were crippled for life who came out of those battles. It was just a terrible tragedy. When you think what America lost in terms of talent and energy and dedication during that World War II, it's almost unbelievable. I am sure that many of the Allied troops were scared, but they were also brave. They realized the cost of fascism and Nazism. They knew it was wrong.

Second, the GI Bill of Rights helped so many veterans. It paid tuition for veterans to go to college. It financed real estate. Many took advantage of these programs and became the backbone of American prosperity after the war. I went into business. I borrowed $25,000 to buy a poultry farm and hatchery. I took advantage of it, and did well at it.

Mary Jane recalled the World War II experience, George leaving to go overseas, and living with her parents:

KW: Where did you live when he went in the service?

MJL:[6] Well, I lived with my parents out in Elmwood, York County. They had a home that was semidetached. They had an extra bedroom, so that's where I stayed when George went to the service. Michael was born when he was out in the Pacific. While George was away, my parents were so happy to have me and the baby at home. They looked out for the baby, and I could go out with my girlfriends. Michael was 6 months old when George returned from the service. I remember my father had a big garden; he came from farming roots so he knew how to make a garden. In those days the government encouraged people to plant a victory garden. He made a beautiful victory garden. He had so many vegetables that he would go all over the neighborhood giving them to people. He tried to raise the things that people would use.

KW: It was fairly common during the war that married men would go off and women would stay home. What was that like, saying goodbye to him and living without him?

MJL: There was always a chance that he wouldn't be back. In fact, I knew people from our high school that had married and the husband was killed. One, in particular, had a little girl, too, that he was waiting to see. He was killed one day before the armistice was signed. It was very sad. Another was a young man who was the president of our class. He was killed too. It was hard on me and George, too. Everybody was in the same boat though. I felt that I couldn't complain because your next-door neighbor had maybe three sons in the service. It happened to almost everybody. I guess you just knew that everybody was in the same boat, and there was no use—you don't complain because your next-door neighbor was maybe much worse off. George returned not long after the bombs were dropped in Japan. It was wonderful to see him again, and of course he was happy to see his son.

Mary Jane further describes their poultry business in which she and George invested money and substantial effort to build into a success shortly after the war:

MJL: He had $25,000 from the government and with it we bought a farm. That was just the down payment. That was Willow Brook farm. We built a hatchery building and had incubators which he bought used. They were in good shape. So that was our start in hatching baby chicks. Now, he had worked briefly for his father, who was also in the baby chick business and learned a great deal. I think his father was a little hurt when we used the G.I. Bill to buy another farm and do the same thing. We had different customers, of course. His father was always very sensible and realistic about things, so he knew that the business would be a good start for us. I used to go out to the incubators and help a great deal. We couldn't afford much help. There were certain things we did on certain days with the eggs that were in the incubators. We would rotate trays so that there would be equal heat on the eggs. I graded the eggs, weighed them, and put them into boxes of 100. For every order of 100 chicks, we gave the customer 102 chicks. I even delivered baby chicks to customers. We had a truck that I drove and took the bulk of them out for sale. I would tell the people how to put them around the stove and what to feed them. Our customers were very satisfied. If they weren't, George would go out to them and see what was wrong and make good on any problems.

Soon, George Leader moved into another career of interest: politics.

State Senator Leader

On returning from the war, George, Mary Jane, and their young child, Michael, took up residence with his parents in York. Leader worked for his father for a time, then borrowing on the GI Bill, established a successful poultry farm. In 1950, he was elected to the Pennsylvania Senate representing York County and succeeding his father. Despite, as George puts it, "quickly becoming bored in the Senate,"[7] he introduced more than 40 bills and served on six committees: Public Health and Welfare, Agriculture, Education, Forests and Waters, Highways, and Insurance.[8] Leader-sponsored legislation included state aid to farmers, research in prevention of poultry and animal disease, fluoridation of public drinking water and other preventive public health measures, establishment of a labor-relations curriculum and scholarships for state-affiliated colleges, creation of rehabilitation programs for alcoholics, and increased state financial support for public education (largely as a result of Republican control of the General Assembly and governor's office, none of the bills were enacted into law).

His most vehement opposition to Republican policy came when Senator Albert Penchan of Ford City introduced a loyalty oath bill on January 15, 1951, during the height of the Cold War, fears of Communism, and the era of Senator Joseph McCarthy. The bill required an oath of allegiance of all state and local officials to the Constitution of the United States and the Constitution of the Commonwealth of Pennsylvania. Leader pointed out that he would agree to take the oath himself. However, he argued that it violated the constitutional rights of educators and religious minorities and that such an oath only served to heighten public suspicion and fear-mongering. Forty-two state senators voted in favor, seven against. Governor John Fine signed the bill into law.[9] Suspicion was aroused that George Leader was a communist sympathizer—or worse, a communist himself—a notion he quickly dismissed as an unfounded Republican tactic to discredit Democrats.

Always ambitious, in 1952 he ran for state treasurer. The commonwealth's Democratic Party had put forth a ticket consisting of Leader, Genevieve Blatt for auditor general, and Judge Guy Bard of Lancaster for U.S. Senate. The likelihood that Democrats would fare well that year was very slim, however. Election returns were decidedly in favor of the Grand Old Party. The commonwealth's vote for Dwight Eisenhower and Richard Nixon totaled 2,415,789, as opposed to Adlai Stevenson's 2,146,269. Moreover, former Governor and Republican Edward Martin was sent back to the U.S. Senate garnering 2,331,034 votes, while his opponent Barr held 2,168,546 (former governor James Duff held the other U.S. Senate seat). Pennsylvania was solidly Republican as both houses of the General Assembly and the offices of governor, internal affairs, auditor general, and attorney general were in the hands of the GOP.[10] Leader was disappointed, but not discouraged, by the result.

He explains his foray into politics in the late 1940s and early 1950s:

KW: What was York County politics like in the 1940s?

GL:[11] There was a strong component in the Democratic Party that was for sale. George Love was a lawyer and county chairman and a good friend of Sam Lewis, the Republican leader. When Sam needed to get somebody elected to suit his purposes, Love would go out and buy up half a dozen Democratic leaders and elect the person Sam Lewis wanted. When I came back from the war, I was elected county chairman at about 28 years old. My father had held the position. I put on a strong drive for registration and put the party together so that it couldn't be splintered anymore. The first election that I chaired, we won every open county and city seat except for one. Then, in 1950, I stepped aside as county chairman to run for Senate and was elected. I quickly grew bored in the Senate, however. The problem is that if you are in the minority party, as I was, you can't accomplish anything. I was usually voting in opposition to the majority viewpoint in Harrisburg. Democrats, especially young ones like me, weren't held in high regard by the Republican powers-that-be. Though I had some important committee assignments, I held no sway.

KW: You ran for state treasurer in 1952. A newspaper article referred to you as an effective veteran campaigner, characteristics that transcended your youth.[12] What do you remember about that campaign?

GL: Yes, I was drafted for that. The Democratic Party was just a shell of a party in those days. To give you an indication, they raised only $60,000 for that whole campaign. Judge Bard from Lancaster left the bench and ran for the U.S. Senate against General (former governor) Martin. I think we bought 15 minutes of radio time in four or five stations around the state, and that's all the electronic media we had. And I don't think we had any print media.

The fact is, Mary Jane lay on the bed and sobbed for a couple of hours when I said I was going to make that run. I initially said I wouldn't run. Mayor Dick Dilworth had called me from Philadelphia; I had told him no, I couldn't do it. It just didn't fit into our financial situation. Mary Jane and I were both working about 60 or 70 hours a week on our poultry farm and hatchery business. Mary Jane knew that if I wasn't there, she would have to work even harder, if that was possible. So, it was not a good time to run. Later on, Judge Bard and Jim Finnegan and people like that called me and talked me into running. Mary Jane was so distraught. I said, "Mary Jane, if you don't do what other people want you to do, sometimes in politics, they may not do for you what you'd like them to do when the time comes that you want to do something in politics." It's a two-way street. I think life is like that also. But, in politics, it's doubly important. If I hadn't run in '52, I certainly would not have been selected as a candidate for governor in '54. And I wouldn't have been able to conduct nearly as good a campaign. I had the—Genevieve and I got the education in that '52 campaign, and it paid off in '54.

So, we campaigned, Genevieve Blatt and I, very hard in 1952; Genevieve for auditor general, myself for state treasurer, and Judge Bard for the United States Senate. Genevieve, the judge, and I lost. The speeches I made, the friends I made, the contacts I made, the knowledge I gained about the state and also about the Democratic Party, meant that I could approach the 1954 campaign from a position of knowledge instead of from a position of total ignorance. Not too many people knew the state from one end to another. Genevieve and I gained tremendous ground in that campaign, despite the loss. We were both young at the time. Remember, I was 34 years old. It was unheard of in state politics for someone that young to run for statewide office! A lot of Republicans thought I was just a young upstart that lacked substance.

Now, of course, Eisenhower was running for president in '52, and he carried the state by several hundred thousand votes. Genevieve, the judge, and I lost the state by about 120,000 votes. Without the coattail effect of Eisenhower, we very well might have won that election. And it was a wonderful experience. It was a very inconvenient time for me to run, to be in a state-wide campaign.

KW: What were some of the issues in that campaign?

GL: One of the big issues when I first got into state politics was Communism. They called all of us liberals, communists. Interestingly, it was a time in our history when most liberals were called communists. When I ran for Senate and state treasurer, some said what a dangerous communist I was! Fortunately, though, it didn't stick. I guess people figured that an ordinary chicken farmer probably wouldn't be a very effective communist. But for a long time, we in the Democratic Party had the curse of the extreme left. You know, (former) Governor Bill Scranton (1963–1967) and I are good friends. Philosophically I don't think we are five degrees apart in terms of where we stand on most issues. He's a moderate Republican, and I'm a moderate Democrat. They never accused him of being a communist. What we need in America is moderation because we can't afford to go to the extreme right or left.

In any case, during the 1952 campaign, Lieutenant Governor Lloyd Wood came to York—my home city, my home county—and said that George Leader's a communist. I don't know for sure but he might have been positioning himself for a run for governor in 1954 and thought that I'd be his opponent. I carried York County in that election so his message didn't carry. And when I ran for governor two years later, I carried the county by 20,000 votes. So I guess they knew he was telling a lie. They knew I wasn't a communist. They knew the Leaders had been landowning farmers for eight generations and paid their bills, and were decent God-fearing people—Christian farmers—and had important positions in the church, and so forth.

KW: You were a vigorous supporter of Adlai Stevenson in 1952 and escorted him through York County during his campaign for the presidency.[13]

GL: Yes, the Leaders were ardent supporters. I liked Adlai. He had substance and was an intellectual. He understood the issues and was a good campaigner. He would have made a good president but he was a perfectionist and that might have harmed him in the office. You can't be a perfectionist and hold high office. You'll be disappointed too much. In any case, yes, I escorted him through York County and later through the state when he ran again. We shared a lot in common.

KW: During McCarthyism and the second Red Scare, Governor John Fine implemented a loyalty oath. What do you remember about that issue?

GL: The General Assembly passed, and Governor Fine signed the Loyalty Oath Bill, as it was called. Realistically, the person behind it was Judge Michael Musmanno from Pittsburgh. I think he probably had been a card-carrying communist back in the bad old days, and he figured the best way to stay out of trouble was to become one of *the* outstanding anticommunists in the United States of America. So he wrote books on the subject, did lectures on the subject, went to all the veterans' organizations, and made speeches on the subject, and he got Senator Penchan from northwestern Pennsylvania to sponsor a bill called the Loyalty Oath Bill. Out of the 50 state senators, only a few had enough backbone to vote against it. I was one of them, and I'm proud of that vote. I said, "William Penn founded this state and he invited people from Germany and Switzerland to come here. Without the Quakers, we wouldn't be here. I wouldn't be sitting here today without William Penn. I won't vote for any bill that's offensive to the founders and that violates the principles of religious freedom and freedom of thought." It was very controversial. It was almost amusing. The four major universities—Pitt, Penn, Temple, and Penn State—sent their leaders to Harrisburg, and they made a deal with the senators. They said they'd police their own and root out suspected communists on campuses. As a result, they secured an amendment exempting them from the bill. Instead of their coming up there with some courage and conviction and honor, and saying, "We're going to protect everybody"—they were satisfied just to protect their own people. Great democracies can do better than that. I think one or two Quaker schoolteachers lost their jobs because they wouldn't sign that Loyalty Oath. I was not a Quaker, but I quickly learned that few in Harrisburg cared about the Quakers. They had quickly forgotten that the Quakers are our hosts here.

There are silkscreen prints in the governor's reception room in the Capitol. They named that series of paintings "The Holy Experiment." I have not forgotten that Pennsylvania is still a holy experiment. In any case, I said publicly that I would take the oath but that we should not subject people to the oath who may violate their spiritual convictions by so doing. I had taken an oath when I went into the military. I had taken an oath when I went into the Senate. I had taken an oath when I served on juries. I had no problem, personally, taking such an oath. The issue to me was imposing on others whose conscience may not enable them to do so. When I became governor, the Loyalty Oath was already on the books. We never rescinded it, but we didn't enforce it. It was hardly enforced, and it was practically unenforceable anyhow.

The next steps for George would be securing the 1954 gubernatorial nomination and, of course, the campaign and election. Mary Jane recalls these events:

MJL:[14] Well, the 1954 election I remember very well. I think the party was pretty well agreed on his candidacy, but a lot of people said he was just a throwaway candidate because nobody knew his name. He had been in the Senate, but that didn't count terribly for him to be known all through the state. Many expected Richardson Dilworth to run. He didn't. Some of the people that got George to run really knew that he was a decent man and that he would be able to serve if he were elected, but they didn't ever expect him to be elected. So he went out and campaigned very hard. Some thought, "Maybe this is the year for Democrats."

I remember one time he was campaigning in Western Pennsylvania. I was with him, but I didn't go too often because we had young children that needed to be tended to. George was giving a speech and pulled out of his pocket a little linen and lace doily about as big as my hand. He said, "Do any of you know what this is for?" Now this is the kind of thing that he did that many other speakers would not have. So he said, "That's a doily to be used with a finger bowl." Now, most of the people he was speaking to had no idea about doilies and finger bowls. So he described that a little more and said that these were the kinds of luxuries that the Republicans had in the governor's mansion in Harrisburg. He would do away with them, he promised. Now the opposition must have had a little trouble with that because he told how much money was spent at the executive mansion for these finger bowls and doilies and how much was spent for other things. Sometimes I was a little embarrassed because I thought, well you know, some people like those little luxuries. But that's the way he campaigned; he made it personal.

Mary Jane remembers, too, that throughout life in politics and business, the Leaders related well to common people, just as George did in campaign speeches, such as the one in Western Pennsylvania in 1954:

> MJL: I had no problem, really, starting a conversation or being friendly with people. I really had no difficulty making friends at all. I knew George had some good friends who helped him financially when he was running for office, and I didn't look down on them or anything, but I just had more in common with the regular people. On one occasion when I was first lady, a group of society women had a lovely tea for me in one of their homes. I knew that the woman who hosted it was very lovely and that her husband was a big banker. They greeted me and we talked, but I never made friends with those people. And I was polite and appreciative, but I wasn't at all interested in their kind of life. George was like that, too. He could talk with and relate to such people, but he had no interest in their lifestyles. We were chicken farmers from simple roots in York County.

Such values would serve George and Mary Jane Leader very well in Pennsylvania's political environment of the 1950s.

Notes

1. See State Historical Marker Program, Pennsylvania Historical and Museum Commission, www.phmc.state.pa.us and Lockman Brian with Dan Cupper and Kenneth C. Wolensky, *World War II Reflections: An Oral History of Pennsylvania's Veterans* (Mechanicsburg, PA: Stackpole Books, 2009).
2. *Pennsylvania Manual*, Volume 92 (Harrisburg: Commonwealth of Pennsylvania, 1955–1956).
3. "Bethlehem Steel: The Rise and Fall of an Industrial Giant," in *Pennsylvania Legacies* 6, no. 2 (November 2006), 10–15.
4. Pennsylvania Cable Network has collected the most comprehensive oral histories of the commonwealth's WWII veterans and published two

related volumes. See Brian Lockman, *World War II—In Their Own Words*, volumes I and II (Camp Hill, PA: Stackpole Books, 2008 and 2009).

5. George M. Leader, *Oral history interview*, August 28, 2009, Hershey, PA, Leader Library and Archives, Dover, PA.

6. Mary Jane Leader, interview with Kenneth C. Wolensky, June 29, 2009, Hershey, PA.

7. George M. Leader, interview with Kenneth C. Wolensky, February 14, 2009, Hershey, PA.

8. *York Gazette and Daily*, Endorsement of George M. Leader. October 31, 1954, 8.

9. Ibid.

10. *Pennsylvania Manual, 1955–1956*, 94.

11. George M. Leader, interview with Kenneth C. Wolensky, February 14, 2009, Hershey, PA.

12. "Leader Seeking Election as State Treasurer: Veteran Campaigner at 34," *York Gazette and Daily*, Sept. 6, 1952, 4.

13. "In Dutch Country," *York Gazette and Daily*, Oct. 31, 1952, 4.

14. Mary Jane Leader, interview with Kenneth C. Wolensky, June 29, 2009, Hershey, PA.

3

The Keystone State's Chief Executive, 1955–1959

Governor Leader tells the story that when he secured the Democratic nomination for governor in 1954, former Philadelphia mayor and U.S. Senator Joseph Clark quipped, "I'm sorry to hear it. George Leader is a nice fellow and I hate to see him be a sacrificial lamb."[1] Clark was reflecting a historic reality in Pennsylvania politics: Democrats seldom fared well in winning the post of chief executive. Prior to Leader, only one Democrat had served in the office in the twentieth century: George Earle (1935–1939) who later changed his allegiance to the Grand Old Party as a result of a dispute with the Roosevelt administration. In fact, during the twentieth century, Republicans have held the governor's office for 72 years, Democrats for 28 years (George Earle, George Leader, David Lawrence, 1959–1963; Milton Shapp, 1971–1977, and Robert P. Casey, 1987–1995).

Leader proved himself as a vigorous campaigner, especially in the concluding months of the 1954 election. Some Democrats, however, expected to lose as was usually the case in Pennsylvania gubernatorial elections. His opponent, Republican Lieutenant Governor Lloyd Wood, had the party machine working in his favor and, early on, appeared to be facing an easy election despite the fact that he wasn't a terribly good orator and, according to Leader, didn't relate well to ordinary people. Leader remained personally upbeat and positive despite that fact that his campaign had to be frugal and spent a modest $240,000 for promotion and advertising. Moreover, his headquarters may have reflected the somewhat doubtful milieu of some in his campaign. Located in a Harrisburg office building, they were described by the *York Gazette and Daily* as "shabby, dark, and underfurnished." While most members of his family supported his goal, Beulah Leader reportedly worried that if her son won, he would be worn by the pressures and demands of public office.[2]

George traveled the commonwealth extensively, often speaking three or four times a day. His mode of transportation was mostly by automobile—sometimes by air—further reflecting the frugality of the campaign. Democrats simply could not afford a high-budget campaign. One of his favorite quotes, expressed publicly, came from William Penn on Pennsylvania as a holy experiment: "There may be room there for such a Holy Experiment, for the nation that wants a precedent, and my God will make it the seed of a nation. That example may be set to the nations, that we may do the things that are truly wise and just."[3] He also stressed the responsibility of citizens to vote and be active in public affairs.[4]

When election returns came in, Leader and his running mate, former state House of Representative's Democratic leader Roy Furman, secured the governorship and lieutenant governor's office by 279,000 votes out of 3.7 million. He won his home county of York by 20,000 votes. Candidates Henry Beitscher of the Progressive Party won 4,471 votes; Louis Dirle of the Socialist Labor Party secured 2,650.[6] Third-party candidates have never fared well in Pennsylvania elections at any level. The victory came as somewhat of a surprise, especially to the Republican establishment as the Grand Old Party had boasted over 2.9 million registrants, compared to the Democrats' number of 2.1 million. Moreover, his victory was held by the largest margin ever secured by a Democratic candidate to that point in state history. He carried 34 counties, a majority of the commonwealth's total of 67. The fact that Leader was, especially, the favorite of the labor movement, such as the International Ladies' Garment Workers Union, no doubt boosted his campaign.[7] Leader had apparently swayed some Republicans with his charisma, promises of professional and clean state government, aid to farmers, education reform, environmental stewardship, and economic development and jobs. Moreover, candidates for the state House of Representatives rode Leader's proverbial coattails: a slim majority went to the Democrats. Yet the State Senate remained under the control of the GOP by one Senate seat.

Time magazine featured the newly elected governor as its cover story on November 15, 1954. Noting the historic results of the election, *Time* said, "That anchor and pride of Republicanism, the great and prosperous state of Pennsylvania, went Democratic—solidly, surprisingly, and in a way that seemed to shatter the pathetic remnants of its once proud and efficient GOP organization." The popular magazine attributed the shift from Republican to Democratic in part to dissatisfaction with rising unemployment in the Keystone State. In some counties, such as in the anthracite region, double-digit unemployment was common in the 1950s as extractive and manufacturing industries slowed significantly.[8]

In the immediate postelection period, Leader received numerous positive editorials from newspapers across the commonwealth. Several editorials pointed out the challenges that lay ahead, including rising unemployment due to a mid-1950s recession and the state budget deficit, yet they expressed confidence in the new governor to address these issues. Theodore A. Serrill, general manager of the Pennsylvania Newspaper Publishers, compiled the editorials and presented them to Governor-elect Leader as a victory memento.[9] The *Pottsville Republican* and *Lancaster New Era* especially noted the challenge of the state budget deficit, particularly as Leader faced Senate Republican opposition to tax increases.[10]

In addition, several newspapers interviewed the governor-elect and his wife at their York County farm, Willow Brook. *Philadelphia Sunday Bulletin* reporter Ruth Seltzer visited the Leaders a few days after the election. Thinking that the governor-elect was busy with state business, she sat down with Mary Jane to ask a few questions about family history and the forthcoming challenges in Harrisburg. Within a short time, George arrived for lunch with Ruth and Mary Jane. The reporter was taken aback when he appeared dressed in "overalls and high brown shoes caked with mud as he had come in from the fields where he had been clearing brush and removing trees." Apparently, this was not quite as becoming of the new governor as she had expected. Also, he did not change his clothes for the meal and graciously exited an hour later to return to the fields.[11]

Wednesday, January 19, 1955, Inauguration Day, was bitterly cold in Harrisburg. Under a clear sky, temperatures dipped into the teens as 35,000 people gathered in front of the State Capitol on 3rd Street to watch George Leader take the oath of office. National news was dominated by President Eisenhower's call to the United Nations to find a solution to fighting between Chinese nationalists and communists. The U.S. Navy's Seventh Fleet stood at the ready to defend Formosa and the Pescadores in the event of attack by Chinese communists.[12] Pennsylvania's focus was, however, on the new governor. In his 15-minute address, Governor Leader promised that the "state's economy was his first concern" as unemployment rates in some areas were in double digits (Leader's commitment to economic revitalization resulted in the Pennsylvania Industrial Development Authority discussed in this chapter). Though new taxes would be unpleasant, he was committed, he said, to raising $500 million in new revenue, over one-half of which would be used to address a growing budget deficit that he blamed on "reckless fiscal policy" of previous Republican administrations. The deficit was estimated at somewhere between 75 to 100 million dollars. New revenue was also needed to fund programs.[13] Governor Leader promised honest, hard-working leadership in Harrisburg. He concluded his address by quoting from Proverbs: "In the Bible on which I took my oath today, these familiar words from Proverbs, Chapter 29, Verse 18 appear: 'Where there is no vision the people perish.' In Pennsylvania, I promise you, there will be vision."[14]

Beulah Leader had tears in her eyes during the address. Mary Jane smiled and had to fix their son Michael's hat on a few occasions. Guy Leader looked on proudly, as did the Leader siblings. At the conclusion of the formal ceremonies, a four-hour parade commenced in which 15,000 marched from the commonwealth. The first family then attended the inaugural ball at the Zembo Mosque in uptown Harrisburg, where 4,500 dignitaries and supporters greeted them. Adding to inaugural uplift, Mr. and Mrs. Marlin Conley of Dover Township, York County, named their newborn son George Leader Conley. Marlin told *The Patriot* that the baby's name was a show of bi-partisan support for his fellow York Countian. The Conleys were registered Republicans.[15] Adding to the excitement of the day, his staff presented him with a large birthday cake, honoring his 37th year.[16]

Leader's first day in office extended for 14 hours. The governor took immediate action to address his concerns about assuring continued leadership in the departments of education and health,[17] and he and Harry Shapiro, the new secretary of welfare, immediately launched an initiative to reform and clean up "miserable conditions" at Allentown State Hospital.[18] Ever concerned about the quality of public health and education, Leader immediately began to search for recognized professionals to lead the Department of Public Instruction (he had accepted the resignation of chief Dr. Francis B. Haas and replaced him temporarily with Dr. Ralph C. Swan of New Bloomfield, Perry County) and Department of Health (where he had appointed an acting secretary of health, Dr. Charles L. Wilbar of Camp Hill, Cumberland County). Swan was replaced with Dr. Charles H. Boehm a year later. He had worked through the ranks of public school administration, having served as a principal, superintendent, and as a chair and member of several education-related commissions. Wilbar's successor was Berwyn F. Mattison, appointed in early February of 1955. Mattison had an extensive career in public health in New York State with experience as a medical educator and in treating tuberculosis. The administration also commenced a review of state accounting procedures, executive branch administrative practices, and personnel operations that led to implementation of professional accounting, budgeting, and personnel management systems housed in a governor's office of administration (the basic elements of such systems lasted well into future administrations).[19] Governor Leader also had to resign his post as a justice of the peace in Dover Township, York County. Although he had served in the post for a few years he never presided over a trial. Of course, it was a post he willingly vacated; he told the Harrisburg's *Patriot* newspaper that he thought the governorship might be more of a challenge, no slight intended for justices of the peace.[20]

In efforts to stave off long-held attitudes and practices in Harrisburg, Leader issued a bold statement to appointees and state employees. He stated, "I detest and will not tolerate laziness and sloppy performance of public duties. This administration will be no hayride for anyone. It is going to be work, hard work. No one in my administration, no matter who he is, is going to draw pay from the state without rendering a fair return in work performed." Moreover, he warned, "It follows that I will be merciless toward corruption and strictly judge offenses against ethics, even if they are within the letter of the law. It is an article of faith with me that government can and will do more."[21] On the other hand, he remained very subtle with regard to enforcing the Pechan Loyalty Oath. He didn't mention anything about it publicly.

Public Policy Reforms

In terms of reform, innovation, and activist public policy, the Leader administration ranks among the top two or three most progressive of the twentieth century, closely competing with that of Republican Gifford Pinchot (1923–1927 and 1931–1935) and Democrats Milton Shapp (1971–1979) and Robert P. Casey (1987–1995). Pursuant to the Pennsylvania Constitution of 1874, governors were limited to one term, though they could hold a second, nonconsecutive term (Gifford Pinchot was the only person to do as such, serving from 1923–1927 and again 1931–1935). In four short years, Leader recorded some major accomplishments, despite the fact that he took the oath of office facing a deficit (the commonwealth's total budget was $1.5 billion) for which he later had no choice but to raise the state sales tax from 1 to 3 percent. Long-term reforms by governors are typically accomplished through legislation. Other initiatives are accomplished by executive order, statement of policy, or regulation. The administration's record and *Acts of the General Assembly from 1955 to 1959* indicate that most of Leader's reforms were accomplished through legislation.[22] Some were implemented through executive order or administration policy statements. Among the major achievements are the following:[23]

- Implementation of the Fair Employment Practices Commission in 1956 to police race-based employment discrimination.[24]
- Employment of minorities: 450 were hired.
- Administrative and policy-based reforms to the commonwealth's mental hospitals including innovative treatments,

adequate professional staffing, facility maintenance, and reducing the institutional population that stood at over 42,000 when he took office.[25]
- Statutory creation of a Governor's Advisory Council on Mental Health.
- Preventive public health measures, especially mass vaccination for polio that was successfully launched by Dr. Jonas Salk and other researchers at the University of Pittsburgh.
- Civil Service reform to expand merit-based selection and promotion.
- Launch of the Hiram G. Andrews State Rehabilitation Center in Johnstown to retrain disabled workers. At its time, the center was the most comprehensive of any publicly funded program in the nation.
- Safety inspection of migrant labor camps by the Department of Labor and Industry.
- Environmental stewardship, including expansion of the state park system, professionalization of forest practices, amendments to mine reclamation law,[26] and greater efficiencies to the practice of leasing oil and gas wells on state-owned land.
- Creation of the Pennsylvania Industrial Development Authority for job creation and expansion of manufacturing.[27]
- Public funding for the education for disabled children.[28]
- Enhanced state aid to public universities and community colleges.
- Launch of agricultural product marketing programs, such as Egg Week, Peach Week, and Apple Week.
- Effective use of federal funds resulting from the 1956 Interstate Highway Act, such as construction of western Pennsylvania's Interstate 79.
- Enhanced statutory capital reserve and surplus requirements for mutual insurance companies to prevent fraud and insolvency.[29]
- Construction of a new State Police Academy at Hershey with state-of-the art programs and facilities.
- Equity in ownership of property, real and personal, for married women.[30]

- Prohibition of the printing and distribution of pornographic adult literature[31] and material in children's comic books that depicted drugs, violence, or vulgar behavior.[32]
- Expansion of the Pennsylvania Historical and Museum Commissions holdings of historic properties.[33]
- Regulation of chiropody, an expanding field of practice in health care.[34]
- Exemption from registration fees and other regulatory exemptions for seeing-eye dogs for the blind.[35]

In addition to legislative and policy accomplishments, Leader made diligent efforts to continually inform the public and communicate his administration's accomplishments to Pennsylvanians, a style highly unusual for Pennsylvania politics. In September 1956, he issued a press release announcing a series of forthcoming reports to citizens to "cover a number of different fields (to) include legislative and administrative accomplishments in various departments of state government." Leader said, "We are going to put out a series of progress reports for the people. It is their state government, and they have a right to know what we are doing for them. It is time that the accent was placed on the positive achievements that have taken place . . . for the welfare of the commonwealth and its people."[36] Leader realized the effectiveness of good public relations and the value of communications in politics.

In managing the affairs of state government and in public policy matters, George Leader was guided by his values. Authors Cooper and Crary write that "while other governors have had strong religious beliefs and values, few have had the courage to stand by them in the face of political and public pressures." A devout Lutheran, "his Christianity was not dogmatic. He was an extremist about virtue, but not about doctrine. Leader was tolerant and accepted all religious beliefs."[37] Also, Governor Leader often said, "It is not enough for any of us to be merely against sin: we must be strenuously, ardently for good. Not only should we be endorsers of good, we must be builders of an ever climbing, always progressive ladder of morality into new, hitherto impossible heights."[38]

The Keystone State's Chief Executive, 1955–1959 / 59

Governor Leader explains the 1954 election and setting out to govern:

> KW: How did you find Pennsylvania's political environment in the early 1950s?
>
> GL:[39] Pennsylvania had been under the influence of the Grand Old Party as least since the Civil War. Now, the Republican Party was a corrupt machine going back to Boise Penrose in the late nineteenth and early twentieth centuries who was the party boss and a U.S. Senator. People like Penrose controlled the party and its purse strings. Now the Democrats weren't innocent by any means. But because the Republicans had been in power so long, their patronage machine was well greased. The state government was riddled with unqualified patronage people in positions that required responsibility. In 1952 Dick Dilworth asked me to run for state treasurer, but I was hesitant as I had used my GI Bill of Rights to borrow $25,000 to buy a poultry farm and hatchery. It was a young business; I just couldn't get away. But they talked me into running. Genevieve Blatt ran for auditor general. We traveled and campaigned together. Eisenhower carried the state by 600,000 votes; Genevieve lost by about 100,000. I lost by a bit more. But there was a strong message that people were voting for candidates and not along party lines. They were at least thinking of change. Maybe they were getting tired of the Republican state establishment. It was an indication that the opposition was more vulnerable than we had originally thought.

Henry Leader, a Yale-trained lawyer who served his brother as legislative secretary, offers his views on the quality of state government in light of patronage:[40]

> HL: It was awful. It was really disgraceful. The whole thing was corrupted. People were in jobs that demanded good service, but they were patronage people—not qualified. State government was a laughing stock. Now, when Gifford Pinchot was governor in the 20s and 30s, he implemented Civil Service and at least tried to clean it up and wean it away from patronage. It was a start, but by the 1950s, it was still pretty bleak. I'll give you an example of how Pennsylvania was looked on. When I was at Yale

Law School in the 1940s, Pennsylvania's Supreme Court decisions were looked upon as a joke. If you were studying an area of law involving a state judicial opinion, the professors would use Pennsylvania as an example to show how bad judicial decisions could be. They were horrible examples of misguided law. It was assumed that when it came to anything involving things like the Pennsylvania Railroad, it was corrupt. There was a joke: a three-judge panel was hearing a case involving the Pennsylvania Railroad that was being sued for some breach or violation. One of judges fell asleep during the proceeding. Another judge nudged him to wake him up and said, "Wake up. They are trying to screw the Pennsylvania Railroad!" In other words, the only time justices paid attention to anything or made key decisions was when the corporations in Pennsylvania were being maligned in some way! Now that's testimony to how powerful the corporate interests were and how corrupt the system was. There was no concern for ordinary people. None whatsoever! It was the corporations who controlled the state government and the judiciary. Everyone knew it. It was accepted practice for at least a century. Well, George promised to change this culture. He said he would change one-party control, chip away at corruption, make government work for the citizens, and give them access to it. Remember, in Pennsylvania gubernatorial politics such ideas were unheard of except for governors like Gifford Pinchot. I guess some people saw George as a revolutionary, maybe a radical.

George Leader further reflects:

KW: In 1954 you secured the nomination for the governor's race.

GL:[41] I'm a pretty positive person, and I had a deep-down feeling that I would win. If you don't have that, it's pretty hard to convey it to others. I campaigned almost every day for eight months. That's a hard schedule; a lot of wear and tear. By the end of the summer, I had really established myself. We spent $250,000 on TV advertising—that wouldn't last you one week today! And we had first-class pollsters. We had a good program to propose. We did a poll on issues. Voters were against a sales tax and for industrial development. Also, Pennsylvania had a lot of strong political bosses in those days, mostly Republican. It was the corrupt Republican machine that was in charge. No one could challenge it. They liked the system the way it was because state patronage was a great thing. But, there was a sentiment among the voters in 1954 to "throw the rascals out." The time had come for us (Democrats) to win.

Leader's election signaled an important and unprecedented shift in state politics and voter registration patterns. In 1956, registered Republicans totaled 2.9 million, while Democrats tallied 2.45 million. By 1960, registered Republicans and Democrats were about even with 2.8 million each. From that point forward, Democrats outpaced Republican registrants well into the twenty-first century. For example, by the mid-1970s Democratic registrants totaled 3.1 million; in 1984, 3.5 million. Republicans, on the other hand, held 2.3 million in 1976, dropping further to 2.1 million by the mid-1980s. Pennsylvania, at least in terms of voter registration, had become a Democratic state with leanings toward the conservative agenda of the party.[42]

State Government: Personnel and Budget Deficits

Immediately after taking the oath of office Leader took action on campaign pledges of reforming state government and on solving the state budget deficit. Professionalizing personnel was a top priority as was raising new sources of revenue that he hoped would come from citizens with higher incomes. He did succeed at civil service expansion and merit selection and promotion of qualified state employees. However, in one of the longest budget stalemates in state history, his proposal for a classified income tax (similar to a graduated income tax) failed in the legislature. Leader was forced to adopt an increase to the state sales tax at a time when the national economy faced recession. He explains his initiatives and the reasons for such action:[43]

> KW: One of your goals was to professionalize state government, making it more responsible to citizens' needs. There were 65,000 individuals employed by the commonwealth during your tenure; Civil Service laws covered 14,000. You expanded coverage by more than 13,000, earning you accolades from some and criticism from others, even in your own party.

GL:[44] That's right. There were some 69,000 state jobs in those days and 80 to 85 percent were patronage. We put about (another) 13,000 under civil service. That was a good start! Governor Pinchot had created the civil service program in the 1920s, but patronage still ruled in Harrisburg. When I came to town, applicants actually had to be qualified to do the work. I remember one time we fired about twenty Democratic Committee people who worked for the state in Philadelphia. They weren't coming to work but were drawing a paycheck. Now some of that happened in previous administrations, but I was determined that it wasn't going to happen to me. I was pretty ruthless about that. When it came to patronage jobs, I was not going to put patronage people in jobs that they weren't qualified to do. And, of course, party loyalists weren't happy with me about it. We put into place a personnel administrator and a job classification system and employees had to meet the qualifications to do the job or they didn't get hired. There were also quite a few politicians who were upset by that, but that was fine with me.

KW: You had to deal with an insolvent state budget for which you proposed a graduated income tax that was opposed by the General Assembly. What do you recall about your disagreement with the General Assembly over taxes and the state budget?

GL: We had significant budget problems when I took office. Governor Fine left me with a large budget deficit. Under the state constitution, Pennsylvania has to balance its budget every year. Expenditures have to meet tax revenue, no exceptions. Well, I proposed a classified or graduated income tax that was intended to tax upper incomes and investment returns at a higher rate than wage earners. A few other states already had income tax systems like the one I proposed. The opposition was vehement and purely political. They knew that if we solved the fiscal problems of the state, then my party would be in a strong position to remain in power for a while. Of course, wealthier people and special interests can and do hire lobbyists to protect their interests. Their interests are, naturally, money and more of it. They don't want to be taxed. Well, we had a stalemate on the issue that lasted several months. The General Assembly and the special interests did their best to embarrass me on the tax issue, and they succeeded. I had to sign a sales tax increase (from 1 percent to 3 percent) to solve the state's budget shortfall. I didn't want to do it but simply had no other choice. As a result, the budget was then balanced, and I could proceed with my programs.

Economic Development and the Pennsylvania Industrial Development Authority [45]

When Leader took office the nation was in the midst of an economic downturn that culminated in what historians have referred to as the Eisenhower recession. Overall, Pennsylvania's unemployment rate was 9 percent. By 1958 it reached nearly 11 percent. In some counties, such as in the anthracite region, double-digit unemployment was common, to say nothing of the level of underemployment that economists did not measure. As were most politicians of the day, Leader was dismayed by the extent of the recession in the Keystone State and made it a priority to do something about it. The single most important economic development bill signed by Governor Leader was the creation of the landmark Pennsylvania Industrial Development Authority (PIDA) (a program reauthorized by subsequent legislation and that continues in existence in the twenty-first century). The program initially provided $5 million in loans through the state Department of Commerce to local and regional industrial development organizations to attract new manufacturing enterprises. One hundred percent of initial capital construction outlays could be financed by a new corporation without any cash up front. Later, state funding was expanded. Specifics of the program were as follows: [46]

- New enterprises could secure a second mortgage loan from the commonwealth for 30 percent of construction or expansion costs. The loan could be amortized over 25 years.
- Fifty percent of capital costs in first mortgage loans had to be borrowed from banks.
- Twenty percent of capital costs had to be secured through low interest loans, referred to as local subscription costs, provided by local economic or industrial development authorities.

Governor Leader reported to the General Assembly that, from 1956 to 1958, 72 manufacturers that made products ranging from military tanks to razor blades to brooms expanded or located in the commonwealth, creating over 60,000 new jobs. The program was promoted and explained nationwide in over 75 newspapers as well as trade journals ranging from *Dunn's Review of Modern Industry* to *Underwear News*.[47] Manufacturers located or expanded in numerous locales, such as Scranton, Windber, Johnstown, Altoona, Wilkes-Barre, Williamsport, Pittsburgh, and Philadelphia. Though it took a national economic recovery and several years to reduce the unemployment rate, PIDA set in place the essential elements to erode the problem.

> KW: You enacted the Pennsylvania Industrial Development Authority (PIDA), a landmark program. Why was this important to you?
>
> GL:[48] PIDA is among the top two or three bills I signed into law. My administration had to decide what the state could do to bring in industrial development to Pennsylvania. Outmigration of people was a real problem in some areas; so was high unemployment. When the coal industry slowed, unemployment rose significantly. One of the things we did was to hold public hearings across the state—Wilkes-Barre, Altoona, and other locales. Now some areas already had their own plans for industrial development, especially in the coal regions. I remember there was a plan in Scranton, called the Scranton Plan, where unions, employers, and developers got together to pool funding to attract industry. Workers were donating pennies from their paychecks to attract jobs. Unions and companies made contributions as well. The idea was that a rising tide would raise all boats. They wanted more above-ground jobs because they had been dependent on coal mining for too long. You know, there is something about the extractive industries, like coal mining, that somehow exploitation seems to be the only word that applies. They don't seem to care about the hospitals or the churches or the community buildings or the infrastructure unless it affects them! Their attitude seemed to be "Get in, get out." Get their money and get out! Now the above-ground industries have a different corporate culture. Not all of them are good or charitable, but many of them want to be a constructive part of the community. So, we held hearings in Altoona, Wilkes-Barre, Erie, and elsewhere on what the state could

do to attract jobs and industry. Out of those hearings came PIDA. It was designed to attract entrepreneurs to distressed areas. If the entrepreneur came up with 50 percent of the financing for a plant or business and the local community could provide the next 20 percent, the state would provide the rest at a low rate of interest. I wanted the commonwealth to provide 100 percent financing. That idea simply wouldn't go over with the Senate Republicans. Later, PIDA was altered in some respects. When we finally got the program through the legislature, it took off beautifully. And, because Pennsylvania had a surplus of unemployed labor, there was no trouble getting workers.

Leader administration officials realized that, even with PIDA, economic recovery would be slow. With regard to workers, Governor Leader promoted several additional initiatives to complement the administration's economic development plan including expansion of unemployment compensation from 26 to 30 weeks and benefit increases from $30 to $35 per week. Other initiatives included opposition to Right-to-Work legislation that Leader said "lowers wages, allows working conditions to deteriorate, and strike viciously at the right of working people to organize," and a firm commitment to veto any anti-labor legislation.[49]

State Hospitals and Mental Health[50]

A preinaugural study of the state's mental hospitals and treatment facilities painted a bleak picture. Lacking professional staff, institutions were overcrowded, did little more than warehouse patients, lacked adequate treatment programs, and had crumbling infrastructure that was questionable for human habitation. Governor Leader and his Secretary of Welfare, Harry Shapiro (a Philadelphia lawyer, former State Senator, and principal architect of the commonwealth's 1930s Mental Health Act that was state-of-the-art at the time, but did not keep pace with growing demands) personally visited each of the 11 mental hospitals (with a total of 39,000 patients) owned by the commonwealth.

The Leader administration implemented "Operation Opportunity" in the fall of 1956 to attract and retain psychiatrists, treatment professionals, and nurses to the commonwealth. Over 2,000 individuals were hired, including nearly 200 psychiatrists, 82 clinical psychologists, 450 psychiatric nurses, and 200 social workers. Henry Leader explained that the mental institutions were ridden with incompetent patronage personnel:

> HL:[51] When George took office, the mental hospitals had *no* trained nurses and *almost* no doctors. If they were lucky, they might have had one part-time doctor for hundreds of patients. It was run on the cheap, favoring all the time a well-established statewide, politically corrupt organization: the Republican Party and its patronage machine. It was simply corrupt. I recall, in one case, we discovered that people were actually paying some Republicans to get and keep jobs at mental institutions. They weren't qualified to work there, but everyone looked the other way. They cheated on people's qualifications; they cheated on the quality of materials; they cheated on the quality of food; and the list goes on. It was a corrupt system perpetuated by the Republican political machine. It just became corrupt from the fact that it was a one-party state for so long. It was rotten through and through, and I don't think George realized how bad it was until he took office. We started to clean it up but it was a huge task.

Governor Leader explains his concerns with regard to mental health in Pennsylvania.

> KW: You were very concerned about the conditions of state hospitals and the treatment of people in them. Why?
>
> GL:[52] Pennsylvania's state mental hospitals were horrible places then. They were medieval. Some people were committed there because they needed help; others were committed for any number of reasons. We had 39 plus thousand people in our mental hospitals, and the number was going up every year. We could hardly build them fast enough—like the prison system now. When people got admitted, there was no treatment. We had entire mental hospitals with one psychiatrist on staff. They were just places to hold people. People were locked away in many cases for life. For example, if a man had grown tired of his wife or if she was going through menopause and he didn't like her behavior, all he had to do was have two physicians certify that she was unstable, and she could be committed. I think hundreds if not thousands of homes were broken

up like that. Any two doctors would sign and put a person away for the rest of their life—didn't even have to examine them. There were a lot of people in mental hospitals who were called "senile." I never heard the term Alzheimer's while I was governor—never once heard that term. The statistics were that anyone who stayed in a mental hospital for over three years was, on average, a resident there for 26 years. That was a life sentence. It was outrageous! I made it a priority to visit every mental hospital in the state. I walked through every ward. I invited state legislators to go along with me to see the conditions. A few did; most didn't. What I found was that there was no treatment. Patients just sat there. They had nothing to do. There were no magazines, no newspapers, no televisions, and no radio. They sat on wooden benches all day. It was ridiculous to be putting people away like we were in Pennsylvania, but we turned it around. We launched a program that soon became the envy of many other states. We called it "Operation Opportunity." Professionals were brought in to treat and care for the mentally ill. Physicians, psychiatrists, nurses, psychologists, counselors, other professionals were hired by the hundreds and went to work in Pennsylvania's mental hospitals. We reduced the population by setting up half-way houses; couldn't just dump people on the street. After several years, the system began to turn around, and the efforts I started were continued by subsequent administrations.

KW: You appointed a Mental Health Advisory Commission to report to you on related issues, treatment options, and policy.

GL: I remember putting the commission in place, although I can't tell you who I appointed. I know we had medical and psychiatric professional people. I wanted to make sure we tapped professionals. Mental health deserves nothing less than professionals. They advised me on many policy and treatment issues that I adopted. New medications, for example, were on the Commission's agenda. There were several new drugs introduced at the time for mental health issues. I don't think it had gotten as far as the modern antidepressants. There were others, though. I seem to recall Thorazine, for example. Also, psychotherapy was something we adopted. The field has come far, but I think still has a ways to go. Mental illness remains a real issue in our society.

Beginning in the mid-1980s Pennsylvania began closing state mental hospitals and, some time before that, moved institutionalized mental health patients to community settings. This was consistent with federal policy that commenced, largely, with the Kennedy administration that provided federal support for community-based mental health facilities rather than government-run hospitals. Pennsylvania's Department of Public Welfare has closed or consolidated a dozen mental hospitals in the last 30 years and reduced the state inpatient population by 70 percent from Leader's time in office. Leader and others note, however, that while the state mental hospital population has been dramatically reduced, Pennsylvania's corrections population has ballooned to nearly 50,000 in the early twenty-first century. One explanation for this growth, according to Governor Leader and many others, is that the mentally ill and those addicted to drugs and alcohol now go to prison rather than to state hospitals.

Pennsylvania's Environment[53]

Expanding state parks and recreation areas, opening additional state lands to hunters, cleaning up strip mines, soil conservation, preventing littering, and expanding state forests were prime environmental programs of the Leader administration. Except for the two administrations of Governor Gifford Pinchot, no governor up to Leader's time had been such an environmental steward. Indeed, in Pennsylvania's twentieth-century political history Pinchot, Leader, Raymond Shafer (1967–1971; Shafer signed sweeping reforms to create Pennsylvania's first environmental superagency, the Department of Environmental Resources) and Robert P. Casey (1987–1995; Casey signed a recycling bill that ranked among the most progressive in the nation and enforced tough restrictions on industrial pollution and out-of-state trash hauling into state landfills) implemented the most sweeping environmental reforms. To Leader, the environment is something to be respected and cared for. His administration is credited for important accomplishments when it came to the environment. He explains:[54]

> KW: You were an environmental governor. Tell me about your interest in the environment.
>
> GL:[55] Well, first of all, that was an era in which we were doing a lot of strip mining. There are whole sections of mountains—for

example between Harrisburg and Scranton—that had been scalped. The trees were gone, the bare ground was showing, the slopes were irregular and steep. You know, there is something about the extractive industries—like coal mining—where exploitation seems to be their goal. They cared nothing about the land and the workers, only about their profits. Their philosophy seemed to be "Get in, get out." Get their profits and get out. Well, this troubled me. I signed a law to require these lands to be cleaned up. The commonwealth required bonds to be put up by the mine operators; either they had to restore the site or the state could draw-down on the bonds. They were, basically, performance bonds. But the strip miners would leave a piece of old machinery on the strip mine and say that they were still excavating; they're still going to mine more coal. In some cases, they avoided carrying out the letter of the law. I was upset about that. I was eighth-generation farm-owning Pennsylvania Dutchman, and to destroy the surface of the earth, not put it back as it was prior to mining, not respect it, and not carry out their contractual relationship on what they're supposed to do really upset me. So I was determined that we were going to do something about it. On top of that, my neighbor in York, Sam Lewis, had become Secretary of Forest and Waters in the previous administration. In the name of economy, Sam Lewis had plowed under two million seedlings that should have been available to plant those areas that had been stripped over. So I was determined we were going to do something different. My administration was going to recruit a professional staff.

KW: Dr. Maurice Goddard was a recognized professional who was a professor in Penn State's forestry school for a number of years. You appointed him as Pennsylvania's environment chief. He served a total of five governors from 1955 to 1979. Tell me about him.

GL: That's right. I had a couple of politicians pushing very hard for the position of Secretary of Forest and Waters, but I kept elbowing them away. I wanted to get a real pro. I didn't know how to do it. One day Genevieve Blatt and I were having lunch. Her brother, Joe, had been a student in the School of Forestry at Penn State. He had graduated. Genevieve said, "You know, my brother always so much admired the man that ran that forestry school at Penn State University." I said, "Really? What's his name?" She said, "His name is Maurice Goddard. I don't know him personally," she said, but, "based on my brother's reactions, he must be great."⁵⁶ Soon after lunch, I called the president at Penn State, Milton Eisenhower, President Eisenhower's brother. I had already called him once before to ask him to release the head of the Department of Animal Industry to become my Secretary of Agriculture. His name was William Henning. He was top-notch, a dear friend of my father's, an honest man, a dedicated man. Among other things he completed putting the entire commonwealth on the federal Soil Conservation Map. That meant Pennsylvania had leadership and participation in the Soil Conservation Program. So, when I called Milton Eisenhower about Maurice Goddard, he said to me, "Who is it this time?" He had already approved Bill Henning. I said, "Maurice Goddard." And he said, "Well you sure know how to pick them." So that was reassuring to me because I really wanted the best, and I didn't have a good background in that field. Except for the kind advice of Genevieve Blatt, I never would have found him. I was so pleased about that. Maurice then came to Harrisburg for an interview. I had gotten in touch with him and asked him to have lunch with me. Following lunch I said, "Where are you going to be the rest of the afternoon?" He said, "I'm going over to Mont Alto to our unit (Penn State's forestry program) over there. I can be reached there." I had already made my choice before he left my office. I called him that afternoon, and I said, "I'd like to select you to be the Secretary of Forest and Waters." He accepted right then and there, and he was just terrific.

Among accomplishments that Governor Leader ranks highly is the efforts of himself and Dr. Maurice Goddard to expand the state park system in the commonwealth. In the fall of 1956, the governor proudly announced that "five new state parks are now in the planning stage. With these additions, we will have brought our total state parks to 51 (an increase of seven, from 44, in 1953) in an intensive effort to accommodate the increasing numbers of people who visit them for recreation. In 1953, approximately 7.4 million people visited them; in 1955, the attendance figures reached 11.5 million. For the benefit of Pennsylvania's sportsmen we increased the amount of state park land that is open to hunting. In 1953, Pennsylvania's sportsmen could hunt 38,000 acres; in 1956, they may use 49,000 acres."⁵⁷ Governor Leader explains the importance of the state parks and other conservation measures:

> KW: You wanted abundant state parks in Pennsylvania.
>
> GL:[58] Maurice Goddard had a sense of social responsibility. In addition, he cared about people just as much as he cared about trees—probably more. One day he came to me and said, "You know the state parks are really a wonderful source of recreation for people of low income. You know if they stay at home they've got to eat. So if they pack their lunch in a basket it doesn't cost them any more. They need half a tank of gas to go to one of our state parks if we have them well-located." There's a tendency for the state parks to be on state land that we already owned. We owned around three million acres at that time. And he said, "We ought to have a park within 25 miles of every citizen of Pennsylvania." Well, he always gave me credit for that idea and I suppose the announcement of that policy came out of my office but really it was Maurice's idea to have those state parks. He said, "A park must have water." We had a park in York County that didn't have water. And he said, "Oh, that doesn't count. You've got to have a park with water." That gave way to the Gifford Pinchot State Park, which did have water. I said, "Why do you have to have water?" Maurice replied "You've got to have something for the kids to do. Water gives you fishing, it gives you boating, and it gives you swimming." He was right about that. You can take kids out on a picnic and they'll enjoy the food of course, but they'll eat the food in a half an hour or so and then what are they going to do the rest of the afternoon or the rest of the day? By having a park with water it really opens up a full range of recreational opportunities. All of the parks that we built had lakes.
>
> KW: You dedicated Gifford Pinchot State Park in York County.[59] Why did you select the name Gifford Pinchot?
>
> GL: My brother Henry and I made the selection. When Gifford Pinchot was governor[60]—and I can remember that because my parents always voted for Gifford Pinchot—one of his policies was simply described by the slogan, "We're going to get the farmers out of the mud." I lived on one of those muddy roads as a boy, and I knew in the spring you had to hitch a couple of horses or a tractor to a model-T Ford truck because the axles were dragging

in the mud. It was a terrible thing to cope with. So Gifford Pinchot, over a period of time and using some of the resources made available by the Roosevelt administration, had paved many of those rural roads. Many of them are still in existence and some of them have been widened and improved. His administration improved six thousands of miles of state roads. As a result, if I remember correctly, Pennsylvania has more state-maintained public roads than all of the New York and New England states put together. The first Pinchot road was built where Pinchot Park is located, and there's a monument there to Gifford Pinchot. We named the park for him. Mrs. Pinchot was still alive. So I said to Maurice Goddard, "Do you know Mrs. Pinchot?" He said, "No, but I know their son Gifford Bryce Pinchot." He got in touch with their son, and through him, we got in touch with Mrs. Pinchot and invited her to come to the groundbreaking. She was in her 80s, which was terribly old to me at the time because I was still in my late 30s. But she was so brilliant. She was one of the most brilliant people I had ever met. She talked about people she had conversed with, either in person or by telephone, all over the world. She ran for Congress three times and lost. She knew scientists, the principal scientists all over the world. She was even more brilliant than Gifford. They, of course, were Republicans. Yet, they were very progressive. By today's standards the Pinchots would be liberal Democrats. We owe Gifford and Cornelia Pinchot a debt of gratitude for moving Pennsylvania into the twentieth century. Old guard Republicans, who hated Pinchot, kept Pennsylvania in the nineteenth century or worse.

KW: You implemented a program advocating forest conservation that, at the same time, trained troubled youth.

GL:[61] The corrections director was Arthur Prasse who started his state career running the institution at Camp Hill when it was an institution for youths who were 15 to 25. It was called White Hill back then. Art did a good job and I promoted him to become commissioner of state prisons later. Pennsylvania had about 7,000 inmates at the time. Now it is over 47,000 and growing. Art came up with the idea of utilizing barrack-like trailers in wooded and rural areas to house delinquent youth and train them in forest conservation, cutting down and planting trees, cleaning up forests and that type of thing. The program moved around the state into various state forests which were under the control of the Secretary of Forests and Waters. Maurice Goddard fully supported the program. Part of our forestry program was called sustained yield, where the state cuts out dead trees, harvests the timber, and keeps trees that have diameters at the base of 12 to 15 inches. That leaves the good trees to come back and harvest later. The old way of slash and burn was outdated. As a result, today the three million plus acres of state forest land are all under careful management by professionals. When I was elected to office I think Pennsylvania had only one or two foresters who had graduated from the Penn State School of Forestry. The commonwealth had a tradition of hiring a lot of political people who didn't know anything about forestry management. Let's face it; it's from those forestry trees that we get our oxygen as they consume CO_2 which is a real danger to our ecology here in America—in the world. Now, when I took over as governor we had 52 percent of the state forested. As a result of some of the programs that we put in to reforest these strip-mined areas, we're now up to 56 percent.

KW: You continued the tradition of Gifford Pinchot in that regard.

GL: We sure did. We didn't have a forestry school in Pennsylvania—in America—until Gifford Pinchot came along in the early twentieth century. As Pennsylvania's commissioner of forestry in the teens and as governor in the 1920s and 1930s (Pinchot was also President Theodore Roosevelt's forestry chief in the U.S. Department of Agriculture), he set up a professional forestry training program at Mont Alto in south-central Pennsylvania. Today it is a Penn State Campus. Pinchot and our forests are real assets to Pennsylvania. We owe him a debt of gratitude. Well, the youth forestry program was a success for the most part. Troubled youth gained important work skills, learned to appreciate nature, and our forests were conserved. I am very proud of that.

KW: Another bill that you signed policed littering, made it illegal, and subjected litterers to fines. This was Pennsylvania's first substantial anti-littering law.[62]

GL:[63] I still feel very strongly on that subject. One time, since being governor, I was following a car from New Jersey that pulled over to the side ahead of me and threw some trash out of the window. So I waited until they got to the first traffic light. They had the window down on the passenger side. I also noticed that they had New Jersey license plates. I put my window down and said, "We don't do that in Pennsylvania!" They were a little startled.

Of course, they didn't go back and pick it up! We always had a lot of littering especially along roadways. Fast food has certainly grown the problem. It was a problem in the 1950s as our highway system expanded. People just didn't seem to care. Just throw it out the window! Let somebody else worry about it. Today, I'm still preaching the gospel of unlittered, clean highways. A lot of people who come from the west—we have a lot of desert as you know in the west—they come into Pennsylvania and they see our forested areas and our highways that go through those forested areas and all that greenery and they say what a beautiful state we have. We need to keep it that way! Isn't that easier than cleaning up the mess afterwards?

KW: What were other major environmental achievements while you were governor that you would like to mention?

GL: Let me expand on soil conservation. As I mentioned, Bill Henning brought the rest of the state under the Soil Conservation Service. I don't know how many million tons of topsoil a year were washing down our rivers into the oceans but it had to be substantial. Soil conservation was really important in those days. I always remember the story of a soil conservationist walking through a field with a father and a son. The son was all ears and wanted to know all about soil conservation and the father was paying very little attention from all appearances. Finally, the father said to the son—the soil conservationist was going to send the son a book on soil conservation that he could study it further—and the father said to the son, "I don't know what you want with that book. We ain't farmin' as good as we know how." I think that attitude sort of started to disappear with the soil conservation program 50 years ago, and we started farming better and did more to preserve soil and save topsoil. We don't realize how precious it is until, perhaps one day, we don't have it. Then we know how precious that topsoil is, because everything that grows has to grow in that topsoil. One time I was looking at some trees with Maurice Goddard and I said, "Oh, I guess those roots go down very deep into the earth." Well some trees send the taproot down many feet. But he took his heel and he dug in the soil and there were the roots of those trees. He said, "Trees grow in the topsoil the same as any other plant." I never forgot that. My administration planted thousands of seedlings in forest lands, in strip-mined areas, and for soil conservation purposes throughout Pennsylvania. I didn't take any of these environmental issues lightly.

Fair Employment Practices Commission (FEPC)[64]

Another Leader milestone was the implementation of Pennsylvania's first significant civil rights legislation, the FEPC. Twenty years in the making, FEPC policed employment-based discrimination based on citizen-driven complaints. Several states and the federal government had implemented similar programs in the late 1940s and 1950s. Pennsylvania lagged behind, no small matter for an important industrial giant. During his campaign, Leader pledged to end such discrimination. Though he faced opposition in the Republican-controlled Senate, political pressure from organized labor and religious organizations and growing support among both Democrats and Republicans provided him with enough support to secure a legislative victory.[65]

> KW: You signed a bill into law for the Fair Employment Practices Commission, the FEPC. This was Pennsylvania's first substantive civil rights bill, ten years before the 1964 Civil Rights Act. Civil Rights and FEPC had been debated in the General Assembly since the early 1930s but no Republican governor would commit himself to signing a civil rights bill. Why did you support FEPC?
>
> GL:[66] I always felt that it was a great disservice to the handicapped and minorities because they couldn't get jobs because of the color of their skin or where they went to church. During the campaign, I committed myself to eliminating such unfair discrimination. Not long after I took the oath of office, my administration submitted legislation to the General Assembly to create the Fair Employment Practices Commission (FEPC). Several other states had such commissions. The federal government had an FEPC. Pennsylvania was behind the times when it came to civil rights. We had a majority of Democrats in the House, and it passed the House rather easily. Then it went to the Senate, of course. And in the Senate, we just didn't have enough votes. The fact is, what the Senate did—they did the very same

thing to me that they had done to preceding administrations on Civil Rights legislation; they just put it back in committee, thus avoiding a floor vote. The Senators brought the bill far enough along that some of them could go on record for or against it, if that seemed to be politically expedient. When the Senate powers that be put it back in committee I was really upset. To respond to this inaction my administration invited about 100 people for lunch at the governor's mansion one day, including Democrats and Republicans, business leaders, labor leaders, community activists, various church and spiritual leaders, and politicians. My strategy was to put pressure on the Senate to act by showing them that we had broad support for FEPC. Out of that 100 we invited probably about 75 accepted which is pretty good for a distinguished group like that because obviously some of them did legitimately have other commitments. We brought them together, and when the Republicans in the Senate heard that we were bringing this group together, they got the FEPC bill out of committee and passed it a day or two before the luncheon was held. Yet, we held the luncheon and two of the most distinguished people there were Republican Senator Andrew Sordoni of Wilkes-Barre and Albert Greenfield from Philadelphia. They were the only two that I individually called on to speak. When I introduced them, I said of Albert Greenfield: "the next speaker is not a Catholic, but he has the highest honor that the Catholic Church in Philadelphia can present to a non-Catholic." Then when I presented Andrew Sordoni, I said, "And now I'm going to present to you a non-Jew who gave the telephone system to the state of Israel." (Sordoni was founder of Commonwealth Telephone Company in suburban and rural Luzerne, Wyoming, and adjacent counties. It was among the state's first small telephone carriers.) The point was to show ecumenical and political support for the bill. The luncheon was a big success. Those people who attended had enough political influence that the Senate passed the legislation upon hearing that they would gather. They passed it with one amendment. That amendment was to outlaw discrimination on the basis of age. That was a good idea, too. I think they made it a better bill. That's the bill that I signed into law.

KW: That was a progressive idea for the mid-1950s.

GL: Yes it was. Remember that it was nearly a decade before Lyndon Johnson signed the Civil Rights Act (1964). I had the first African American in my cabinet that had ever been in a cabinet in Pennsylvania or any governor's cabinet anywhere in the nation. His name was Andrew Bradley from western Pennsylvania. He was one of my early supporters and a dear friend. After I signed the law he said to me, "Governor, there are two things we need as a minority. We need the right to vote, and we have that. We need the right to employment, and you have given us that. Those are the two things we really need." He overlooked one thing. If he were living today I think he would agree with what I'm about to say. They also need the right to education—to a good education, including higher education—because we live in a society where if you don't get an education there's a ceiling on what you can do with your life. I have a saying: If you are over 30, I don't care what letters you have behind your name, I want to know—*What can you do*? But that's not generally true in our state or in our nation. The letters behind your name many times either open a door for you or the lack of those letters keeps the door closed.

Education for Handicapped Children[67]

Of all of his legislative and policy accomplishments Leader consistently points out that his most significant was a mandate that all public schools provide education for handicapped children (contemporarily referred to as special needs children). Leader explains that at least part of his interest in this issue came from personal experience that enhanced his awareness of the needs of such children:

> KW: Some of the curriculum standards were changed and what was referred to then as special education for blind and handicapped children was established by your administration.[68]
>
> GL:[69] This was *the* most important bill I signed into law in my opinion. Well, I'm going to take credit for special education, and maybe God prepares us for some of these things because we had a blind son (Fred Leader) so I was very conscious of handicapped children. We called in Dr. Gross who was in charge of special education at the Department of Public Instruction. My brother Henry and I sat down with Dr. Gross. Henry, who was serving

as my legislative secretary, had been the attorney for two or three school districts, so he knew the school code like the back of his hand. Back in those days the state, by law, contributed 51 percent of the money for the public school system. Today they're putting up about 37 percent, or even less, which has contributed to the large increases in property taxes. In those days, the state had to put up 51 percent. I said to Dr. Gross, "Suppose we established programs for the handicapped and then billed the school districts for their 49 percent." He said, "Well that would be wonderful." I looked at my brother Henry and said, "Would that be hard to draft into legislation?" He said, "No, that would be a very simple amendment to the school code." So I said, "Do it." So we put it in a bill, and in two or three months, I signed that bill into law. It said that school districts must provide education for the handicapped, crippled, and retarded or the state would do it and bill the school district for their 49 percent. I should also mention that the state pension for blind citizens was increased from $50 to $60 per month. So we helped blind people as well. In any case, the number of students in special education went—in about five years—from 50,000 to 250,000. I think it was a major accomplishment of my lifetime.

Public Health and Polio[70]

By most measures poliomyelitis ranked as the No. 1 public health threat in the 1950s. Public fears were heightened as the disease spread particularly in summer months through such venues as public pools, swimming holes, and other public places where person-to-person contact was high. University of Pittsburgh scientists, with Dr. Jonas Salk at the lead, experimented with various vaccines and achieved success by the mid-1950s. The polio vaccine and its widespread use was probably the most significant public health achievement of the era. Governor Leader explains the polio vaccine and other public health initiatives during his term in Harrisburg:

> KW: Polio was an epidemic in our society in the early-to-mid-twentieth century. What do you remember about the polio epidemic and the vaccination?

GL:[71] Polio was very frightening. It was more or less in the summer months that children were the most vulnerable. Of course, adults could get it too. It was associated with swimming in swimming holes, as they put it in those days. We didn't have a lot of swimming pools, but we had creeks and rivers and swimming holes that were mostly quarry holes. Everybody was afraid that those were places where polio might be transmitted. There was an Australian nurse—they called the nurses "Sisters" in Australia. Her name was Sister Kenny and she came up with a treatment for polio based on hot towels. The moist heat would help the victims of polio to make a better recovery. While I was governor, Doctor Jonas Salk and his fellow researchers at the University of Pittsburgh developed a vaccine. All of the members of my family were vaccinated. Many people received those shots. People were so excited because a good many of the scientists said that it couldn't be done. Salk is quoted as having said: "It's amazing how many of those people who said it couldn't be done—those scientists who said it couldn't be done—it was amazing how many of them said, 'Well I knew all along that Jonas Salk was going to come up with something' or 'Somebody would come up with something.'" So they changed their tune. It's a good lesson in what Jonas Salk did in light of the fact that he had little support in the scientific community and went on faith that he could conquer this dreaded disease. He saved a lot of lives. We brought him to Harrisburg and had a joint session of the legislature. He appeared before that joint session and we conferred on him the Pennsylvania Medal for what he had achieved. I wanted to do something more substantial, so the commonwealth committed itself to endowing a chair at the University of Pittsburgh. Since chairs were not ordinarily dedicated to living individuals, it was called the Commonwealth Chair at first, with the idea that at the appropriate time it would be renamed the Jonas Salk Chair of Preventive Medicine.

KW: On another health-care related question, you launched the Hiram G. Andrews Vocational Rehabilitation Center in Johnstown. What do you remember about vocational rehabilitation in the 1950s?

GL: It was a new idea. We had done a little of it in this state, but very little. Hiram Andrews was the minority leader in the House, a Democrat of course, for many years. He was from the Johnstown and Altoona area; a very bright guy. He was a newspaper man, a journalist. He had a great gift in being able to express himself. He was a wonderful debater. I think the Republican leaders thought it would be nice to do something for Hiram because he reciprocated in some fashion by supporting something they needed. So they began that project out there, and they gave the job to the lowest bidders. Well when you do that, if you don't prequalify the bidders, you sometimes get some very bad contractors. I always said, "The biggest crook can always be the lowest bidder because he'll make it up on change orders. He'll make his profits on his change orders." The building out there was in the hands of a very incompetent contractor. Some of the walls were so bad that they had to be torn out and the concrete repoured. But eventually the project was finished and it became a modern rehabilitation center. It did some real good.

KW: Also related to public health, you vetoed Act 5 of 1957[72] —a liquor law. The law would have exempted already licensed alcohol retailers going through state inspections when they applied for relicensure. At the time, you wanted retailers to go through a thorough inspection and show compliance with all regulations, such as closing on Sundays, prior to having a license renewed.

GL: Yes, that was particularly important in areas where they tended to ignore the laws. Some said they were closed on Sundays but they were really open. Pennsylvania is a religious state and the law was that, with very few exceptions, bars had to be closed on Sunday, a day traditionally dedicated to worship and family time. Some bars ignored laws against being open on Sunday, serving minors and staying open after hours. Others broke laws in more serious ways. Alcohol consumption and alcoholism were, and are, real social problems—like an epidemic. We've always had alcoholics, just as we always will have people who are gambling addicts, sex addicts, money addicts, drug addicts. There are addictions in all fields. Back then they told me that some of the bars could not survive without the alcoholics that come in at 7 o'clock in the morning or 8 o'clock in the morning to get their couple of shots to get going. So, I wanted those places regulated as closely as possible. They had to comply with the law or lose their license. They had to be closed when state law said they had to be closed. They had to be properly inspected and licensed.

Transportation Infrastructure

President Eisenhower signed the National Interstate and Defense Highways Act (Public Law 84-627) in 1956. Initially the bill allocated over $25 billion for the construction of 41,000 miles of highway in what is among the largest public works projects in American history. As a result of consistent construction for over 50 years, by the early twenty-first century, Pennsylvania's interstates encompassed 12 primary routes and 11 auxiliary routes. Such highways comprised a total of nearly 1,800 miles carrying 24 percent of all vehicle traffic annually. With federal aid, the interstate highway system in Pennsylvania commenced with Governor Leader's term in office. He explains:

> KW: Governor, what do you remember about building and expanding the interstate highway system?
>
> GL:[73] Even before the passage of federal law for the interstate highway system, I had committed myself and my campaign of 1954 to put a superhighway across northern Pennsylvania—east to west—and to put one north and south in the western part of the state, connecting the West Virginia Turnpike to the Erie Thruway. Of course, the system would be greatly expanded, but these roadways were ones that I felt I could commit to in my time in office, especially when the federal government was going to provide funding through the Eisenhower interstate highway bill. Interstate 80, the east-west route, was begun in the early-to-mid 1960s and fully opened a few years later. Interstate 79 in western Pennsylvania was a different story. The Erie Thruway in Pennsylvania connected with the New York Thruway, which ran all the way across southern New York State. It was a fine road, but there was no good connecting link going south from New York Thruway. The West Virginia Turnpike was a total financial disaster. The bonds were selling for 60 cents on the dollar. They couldn't generate enough money to pay the interest on the bonds. They were in default at times. When I was campaigning for governor, I committed myself to build what became I-79. After I was elected we brought the experts in to work on a traffic count and found that only a short segment of 30 or 40 miles west of Pittsburgh would have generated enough traffic to carry the interest on the

bonds. It wasn't too long, about a year or two, until the Eisenhower administration came up with the interstate program. In fact, U.S. Senator Albert Gore, Sr. (D-Tennessee) was a prime sponsor of the federal Interstate Highway Act that Eisenhower signed.[74] So, it was a bipartisan effort. We had no trouble getting funding for Interstate 80. But the road that was going to connect the Erie Thruway to the West Virginia Turnpike was a real problem. We worked on it for months and months. The people in Washington just didn't see the virtue of it. I had to call in a big name to help me get the funding for I-79: General Richard K. Mellon, who was *the* Mr. Mellon of that generation. The Mellons controlled U.S. Steel, Gulf Oil, and many other companies. Richard liked to play soldier. I guess it was stress relief. So, he would spend two weeks with our National Guard in Indiantown Gap every summer. He'd put on Marine field shoes and a uniform and he was General Richard K. Mellon for two weeks. He was a very modest man, a very nice man. My Adjutant General was Anthony J. Drexel Biddle. Tony said, "I'd like to bring General Mellon up to your house for a drink some afternoon." And I said, "That would be fine, but first we got to find out what he drinks because we don't keep alcoholic beverages in the mansion." So he did and they came up, and General Mellon and General Biddle and I sat in the drawing room to visit over a drink. In any event, I knew that the Mellon people really cared about western Pennsylvania, and when Richard K. Mellon came back from the service, he set up the Allegheny Conference, which spent a lot of money in planning and working out the various needs of western Pennsylvania, at a time when Pittsburgh was considered a dirty, smoky city and probably one of the least desirable places to live in the whole state and, for that matter, probably in the whole United States. So he was working in the direction of making it attractive. I said, "General Mellon, there's something you could do for western Pennsylvania that would really be great for them—for that part of the state." He said, "Well, what is it?" I said, "You could help me get a four-lane highway from Erie to the West Virginia Turnpike. It would be great north-south circulation for your part of the state." He was very polite about it, but he didn't say he would or wouldn't do it. He was just very polite about it. I think it was only a couple of months after that when the road was put on the interstate program, and that is now I-79 and a very, very useful road to Pennsylvania. I'm sure Richard K.

Mellon played an important role with Congress and the federal government in getting approval for I-79 but I never knew the details of what he did. The road is a great asset. I had always hoped to name it for him, but Governor Ray Shafer decided to name part of it up there on his end of the state. Ray came from up around the Meadville area, so he named part of that for himself. I couldn't do what I wanted to do and name that road the Richard K. Mellon Highway.

Social Issues: The Death Penalty, Abortion, and Women's Rights

In oral history interviews Governor Leader was asked about several social issues—and his response to them while in office—that grew in controversy in the latter half of the twentieth century.

> KW: Governor, I want to ask you about at least two controversial issues that have been around for a long time in politics. First, the death penalty. There were death warrants signed throughout the 1950s and there were some executions. In fact, Pennsylvania Department of Corrections statistics indicate that 11 executions were carried out by electrocution at Rockview State Correctional Institution during the Leader administration. What do you remember about the issue of the death penalty when you were governor? And how did you approach the signing of death warrants and executions?[75]
>
> GL:[76] Well, I tried to—I tried to do it without thinking about it too much. At one point I said I will never run for governor again as long as we have the death penalty.
>
> KW: Did you say that publicly?
>
> GL: No, I don't think so. It was not a public issue and I didn't make it an issue. It was taken for granted that the state had an obligation to execute those convicted of capital crimes such as murder. Right now some of the states are outlawing the death penalty. Inhumane treatment is an issue. Costs are an issue. Appeals for 5, 10, 15 years that it's very costly to carry out. Sometimes it is hard for the state to sustain a conviction without a death sentence being overturned or seriously challenged. Then, of

course, there is the psychological cost of actually carrying it out. It affects everyone involved, not just the inmate. I am now totally against the death penalty for one very good reason, at least. That is that we seem to think that when we fragment the responsibility from the prosecutor, to the jury, to the judge, to the appeals courts, and so forth down the line to finally the governor—what the governor actually does is assign the date—we seem to think when we fragment the process we somehow obliterate what the Bible says in the Ten Commandments. It tells us that "We shall not kill." I do not want to have the authority over another man's life ever, ever again.

KW: I want to ask you about abortion and, on a related social welfare issue, you vetoed Act 23 of 1957[77] that would have garnished the wages of parents who were delinquent in paying child support, because you said the bill would have unfairly extended the time period in which wages could have been garnished from 30 days to 60 days. You didn't agree with that. You thought wages should be garnered within 30 days. Later, you signed a bill with that provision. What do you remember about that in addition to abortion?

GL: First, I hardly ever remember abortion being discussed or mentioned either in my campaign or while I was in office. It wasn't talked about. It wasn't discussed. It certainly happened but no one mentioned it. Maybe they were afraid? I remember rumors about a doctor in Harrisburg who performed abortions. But that's about it. Abortion didn't become an issue until the *Roe v. Wade* era. One of the things that people who object to abortion seem to overlook, at least in part, is the responsibility of the father of that embryo. I think there's a high percentage of fathers of children out-of-wedlock who never, ever take any responsibility for that child, for the support of that child, for the parenting of that child. That's one of the reasons I think that women should have control of their own bodies. They should be permitted to make their decision since, in some cases, the fathers don't care. I don't like abortion any better than anybody else, but I don't think the government should make the decision for that woman. I think she should be permitted to make her decision. Now, related to that, is parental responsibility to support a child after birth. In some cases, fathers are absent because of divorce, separation, or because they were never involved in the woman's pregnancy or the child's life to start with. The commonwealth has to have a program that would require the fathers of those children to pay for their support or any parent or guardian who is delinquent in paying child support to own up to their responsibilities. Anything that made it easier for fathers to get away from their responsibilities I was and continue to be against. Therefore, they had to pay child support in a timely manner. Extending it beyond 30 days was unreasonable, I thought. I hope it helped some children. Maybe if there was adequate support for children in the first place, we wouldn't have so many abortions. Parents and guardians have a responsibility to them. So does government, the schools, the citizenry, and others. Government has a duty to uphold those responsibilities.

KW: You signed Act 417 of 1957[78] giving women equal property rights. Why was this an issue?

GL: Yes, I remember we had a series of bills on women's rights. Not many passed, but that was one of the ones that did. I'm very proud of that. The problem was that if a couple was divorced, by law the female did not have equal property rights. In other words real estate and other property could go right to the man. In addition, if there was no will when a husband died, the women again had no legal right to property. It is hard to believe that women fought hard to get the right to vote in 1920, but in Pennsylvania they did not have legal property rights! So, I signed that bill to give women equal property rights and end a long-standing injustice. I really don't remember much opposition to that bill although I am sure that some of the Republicans didn't agree.

KW: You also signed into law two important bills related to literature. One of them regulated comic books.[79] Comic books, purchased mostly by children, were prohibited from having lewd or risqué material and anything that promoted narcotics or alcohol. A related bill prohibited adult literature published or sold in Pennsylvania from having "filthy, indecent, disgusting, obscene or other material."[80] It was a bill to regulate pornography.

GL: Pennsylvania is a pretty religious state. Maybe not necessarily all of the people are churched but many have high principles, especially in the rural areas. Those ideas were reflected in that legislation. I'm sure that there were groups—church groups and groups of high moral standing—that pushed for that legislation, and I was glad to sign it. I do think planting bad seeds in the minds of children is a very devastating and dangerous thing. Maybe that sounds conservative by today's standards, but I— I'm not a book burner, and I detest the people that are. But I do think it's all right to see the children get reasonably clean, moral literature. And comic books were read by a lot of children—and adults, too.

Other Public Policy Issues: Civil Defense, Higher Education

The Cold War was a major political issue during the 1950s. Fear of a Soviet nuclear attack, culminating in the Cuban Missile Crisis during the Kennedy administration (1961–1963) was very real. States implemented or expanded civil defense programs to educate and protect citizens in the event of a nuclear or conventional military attack. Fallout shelters were common, as were drills in schools such as "duck and cover." In a speech at the Governor's Conference on Fitness, Leader explained the Cold War environment: "Soviet Russia had put a satellite into space. The tension of the international fencing match is mounting, and it has appeared that the best Americans could do was to parry and try to hold ground." Leader continued: "(when) Sputnik had been launched, the great crisis of intellectual education was at hand, calling for prompt and careful resolution." Among the answers to the Soviet challenge that Leader espoused was physical education and fitness among Pennsylvania's youth in order that schools "upgrade the health and physical condition of every child in the commonwealth and to teach him how to keep that health through adulthood into advanced age."[81]

> KW: The Cold War was a major issue in the 1950s. You implemented some Civil Defense measures such as expansion of fallout shelters, training for high school students on first aid, and development of Department of Health regulations and education campaign to guard citizens against radiation exposure.[82] What do you remember about the threat of nuclear war during your time as Governor?

GL:[83] I didn't really think about it. I didn't worry about it because I let the people in Civil Defense worry about it. It was a time in our country when there was a lot of fear. When I was governor, the Pennsylvania National Guard was held in very high regard and was prepared to be called up if it was needed quickly because of nuclear war. Yet, I hate to think of the many billions of dollars we spent on fallout shelters and the like. When I think of the foolishness of trying to have a bomb shelter against the kind of attack the Soviet Union would have been able to muster—it just goes to show how stupid we can be even in high places.

KW: That brings us to another related subject. When you were governor you also implemented the beginnings of the community college system in Pennsylvania.

GL: Yes, I did. Remember, that was a time when politicians said America should educate people to compete against the Soviets technologically and in science. When I was a teenager, the first girl that I was a little sweet on in high school suddenly disappeared. I said, "What happened to Gladys Innerst?" I found out that she went out to live with her sister in California. Her father owned the Ford agency in Jacobus, Pennsylvania. She was a lovely girl. She went to live with her sister in California. Why did she do that? Well, if she went out there for her senior year in high school, she could get a free two-year junior college education. This was in the Depression, and people didn't have money for a lot of things in those days, especially higher education. Even the Ford dealerships were in trouble, in most cases, because Henry Ford unloaded a lot of Model Ts on them and made them pay for them so that he could use up all the parts he had stored in his warehouses. So, I learned that California has free college education for all their students who finished high school. I thought that was a terrific idea. I often wonder if it was the liberal use of higher education in California that permitted them to have the development of the computer industry in California, such as the Silicon Valley. Maybe if we had done it in Pennsylvania it would have been the "Susquehanna Valley" that had the great leap forward in the use of computers. Remember that the first computer ever built was built at the University of Pennsylvania, and I've seen that piece of equipment (ENIAC was developed in the early 1950s).[84] It was a remarkable achievement. I'm sure the Soviets knew about it. If you give your citizens a great foundation in education, a good many things can follow. When I got to be governor, I couldn't wait to put in legislation on junior colleges, community colleges. To show that I was sincere, I had to show where the money was going to come from. Back in those days, a soda sold for 5 cents for a bottle. If you wanted to take the bottle along, you had to pay 2 cents deposit. When you brought the bottle back, you got your deposit back. I recommended a penny tax on soda to pay for college costs. I said if a kid isn't willing to pay a penny more for soda in order to get a free college education—or a cheap college education at least—then they don't deserve it. Well, I didn't realize that the Association of Soft Drink Manufacturers in Pennsylvania had a Senator on their side who opposed a penny tax on soda; because of that, the penny tax bill wasn't passed. Maybe it wouldn't have passed, but I blame myself for recommending that tax—showing where the money was going to come from. However, if I hadn't shown where the money was going to come from, that in itself might have defeated it also because the General Assembly was very budget conscious. The bill passed the House; it didn't pass the Senate. It was two or three administrations later, I think, Governor Scranton might have signed it. So I gave Governor Scranton a wonderful idea.

Gubernatorial Vetoes and Opposition to Special Interests

As in advocating for reforms and progressive public policy where he thought necessary, Leader was not reticent to oppose policy and legislative proposals, especially those promoted by special interests to the detriment of ordinary people. Two examples are deferrals for corporations in paying taxes and a bill that would have, in his view, made coal mines more dangerous, while benefiting the coal industry.

In 1955, Leader vetoed a Republican-sponsored bill that would have enabled corporations to defer payment of capital stock and franchise taxes, as well as corporate net income taxes. Leader especially saw fit to veto the legislation as it was promoted by the same political forces who opposed him on implementing a graduated income tax. Corporations had to pay their fair share in a timely manner, according to the governor, especially since common taxpayers did not have the benefit of a deferral and since the commonwealth desperately needed the revenue. He explains:

> KW: You vetoed a lenient corporate tax measure. Corporations would have been permitted to defer their capital stock and franchise and income taxes or choose alternative methods of reporting income that would have resulted in them paying lesser taxes.[85]
>
> GL:[86] That's right. It's always been a big issue with the Republicans to support reducing taxes on business; and there is a lot to be said for that. One of the problems, still today, is that many businesses are Subchapter S corporations. And Subchapter S corporations don't pay their income tax directly. They generally pass the money through to their stockholders who have to pay the tax. In any case, I vetoed a measure that would have allowed corporations to defer tax payments. Why should they be permitted to do so when individuals cannot? Of course, I was opposed on this by powerful lobbyists like the Pennsylvania Manufacturers Association. That was fine with me. I don't know if corporations still pay their fair share in this country. Many use tax shelters, like registering in the Cayman Islands. Others probably do pay their fair share. But the ones that are international companies that can slough it off because they pay income tax in foreign countries at a much lower rate—they do not pay their share. The ones who really pay their share do not use the obvious tax shelters. Some wealthy people, too, keep deposits in Swiss and foreign banks to avoid taxes. None of this is fair to the ordinary taxpayers.

In an amendment to the commonwealth's deep coal mining laws, the coal industry wanted statutory permission to store certain volatile gases, such as tanks of oxygen and acetylene, inside coal mines. The bill allowed only the industry to set standards for the transportation into and throughout the mines and their storage. Leader vehemently opposed such an amendment. The mines were dangerous enough and too many lives had been lost in explosions, fires, cave-ins, and floods.[87]

KW: Explain your veto of a bill that would have granted the coal industry carte blanche with regard to storage of volatile gases in coal mines.

GL:[88] There was all too little safety in mining over the years. I'm always reminded of the power of the coal industry when I drive Interstate 81 through Schuylkill and Luzerne Counties. I see an exit sign there for the town of Delano. My favorite president was Franklin Delano Roosevelt. His mother was a Delano. The Delanos had a lot of money. And they made some of it by mining anthracite coal in Pennsylvania in a time when coal miners were dying right and left from miner's asthma, dust, very poor air circulation, and so forth. Not only the Delano family, but many corporations and families, became very wealthy off of Pennsylvania coal, while the miners and their families were destitute. I was angry about this. Well, the coal industry wanted legal approval to determine what they could store in coal mines to make it more convenient for them and reduce shipping and storage costs. They wanted to store acetylene, oxygen, and gases that are very explosive. We had already had quite a few mining explosions. I simply said no. I wasn't going to put miners' lives at stake for the convenience of the coal companies. The mining industry was a powerful lobby back then. They wanted the bill. The United Mine Workers union was a powerful group, too. They opposed the bill. I am glad to say I sided with them. They certainly were very active in Pennsylvania legislature in those days.

The Leader Term Comes to an End

In January 1959, Pittsburgh Mayor and well-respected Democratic politician David Lawrence was sworn in as the commonwealth's new governor. Lawrence had been a statewide influence at least since the administration of George Earle where he served in key positions and was an important advisor to Earle. In addition, Lawrence and Leader were allies in Democratic policy, though they didn't always get along. When Lawrence became governor, it was time for the Leaders to return to private life; though George never expected to fully retire from politics. While he considered but didn't pursue high office again, he remained active in public policy issues as discussed in coming chapters.

As Governor Leader prepared to depart office, he proudly explained the administration's accomplishments to the General Assembly, the press, and the public:

> We acted in the fields of social progress, the things of humane concern such as public health, the care of the mentally retarded and the mentally ill, and the advancement of public education. We acted to conserve and develop for our wise use the natural resources of our state to purify its streams and to increase its opportunities for outdoor recreations. No program can be effectively carried out unless we have first-rate people in jobs which call for special training or special skills. And, so, this administration has tried to build a trained corps of technological and professional personnel, selected by merit, and protected in their careers. One out of five Pennsylvanians still lives in an area of chronic labor surplus. Joblessness was a problem when I took office. PIDA has helped, but there is still more to be done. This is a great state. Great in its resources, great in its industrial might, great in its people. I have emerged from these four years with unbounded confidence in our future. I predict that it will become greater still in the years to come. It is with that certainty that I wish you well in your direction of this commonwealth we love so deeply.[89]

By most accounts, the Leader administration set out to accomplish what the governor had intended. According to the Harrisburg *Patriot*, "Leader was a true-believing, highly idealistic liberal who was willing to buck-the-tide and take the consequences in a conservative state. The Leader administration was exciting and controversial politically, legislatively, and intellectually. It was an administration that could trip over hills but move mountains. In achievements, it ranks with the best administrations in state history."[90]

Besides his administration's policy and legislative accomplishments, one of the most complimentary views on Leader's political legacy came some years later when the Harrisburg *Patriot* ran a series on Pennsylvania's chief executives: "Because of Leader, the modern Democrats in Pennsylvania came of age. Leader helped make them respectable and responsible. Perhaps his lasting reputation will lie in his helping make Pennsylvania a two-party state.

Next to Maine and Vermont, Pennsylvania has been the most consistently Republican state in the nation. After Leader, this was no more."[91]

The Philadelphia Inquirer wasn't quite so kind, however. In fact, their evaluation was the opposite of the *Patriot* and left the Governor scratching his head at its bluntness: "Leader had nothing perceptible to offer the people of Pennsylvania but one of the worst records as Governor ever produced at Harrisburg." Opining on his unsuccessful campaign for the U.S. Senate (see chapter 4) the *Inquirer* said, "We do not want hack politicians bereft of ideas and imagination, who aspire to higher office merely as another stepping stone in a political career without any slightest qualification for the post."[92] Governor Leader didn't respond to the harsh criticism. "That's politics,"[93] he later said.

Mary Jane Leader reflected fondly on their time in public life in Harrisburg:

> MJL:[94] They were happy days. We met many interesting people from all walks of life. One of my jobs was to host teas for almost any Pennsylvania group that was in Harrisburg at the time. I would greet them, shake hands with everybody, and have tea for them at the mansion (Keystone Hall on Front Street in Harrisburg). We also had young children, which was unusual for Pennsylvania's governors.[95] First ladies weren't supposed to be outspoken on issues back then. Not many women were even involved in politics. First ladies were supposed to be more formal—host teas, things like that. I really wasn't very outspoken, but I didn't always accept that I shouldn't be involved. Eleanor Roosevelt broke that mold, but I still had to be careful because Pennsylvania wasn't accustomed to that kind of thing. One of the issues that George cared a great deal about was mental health, and I supported him in this matter. Mental health probably created more buzz than anything else because people misunderstood a lot about it. George felt that there were a lot of people in the mental hospitals that really should have had advice, treatment, and drugs to help them. It seemed that if somebody in the neighborhood acted differently, people suspected he had a problem, and they put him away. George was so opposed to putting people away. He opposed locking the door and keeping them there. He felt that we should know a lot more about the

person and their problems and help them get back on track. He was always looking out for people that nobody cares about. He still is. I supported him on that and continue to do so. It was an exciting time when he was governor; very fulfilling years. They went by very quickly. Sometimes it is hard to be in the public spotlight as we were for several years. I was really happy to get home with family again and be able to just relax, not be in the spotlight, and not have to think about what I was going to say for fear it would be mistaken or somebody would get another idea for it. It was just nice to get back to family. We went back to York County, back into farming and the poultry business. It was time to move on.

Notes

1. George M. Leader, interview with Kenneth C. Wolensky, January 31, 2009 Hershey, PA, Wolensky, "Born a Leader," *Pennsylvania Heritage*, Winter, 2002.

2. *York Gazette and Daily*, November 1, 1954, p. 2.

3. Richard Cooper and Ryland Crary. *The Politics of Progress: Governor Leader's Administration, 1955-1959* (Harrisburg, PA: Penn's Valley Publishers, 1982). p.6.

4. "Leader Stresses Citizen Responsibility as 150 Hail Candidate in York County," *The York Dispatch*, May 2, 1954, p. 2.

5. Mary Jane Leader, interview with Kenneth C. Wolensky, June 29, 2009, Hershey, PA.

6. *Pennsylvania Manual*, 1956.

7. Kenneth C. Wolensky, Robert P. Wolensky, and Nicole H. Wolensky. *Fighting for the Union Label* (University Park: Pennsylvania State University Press, 2002).

8. *Time*, November 15, 1954.

9. Correspondence from Theodore A. Serrill to governor-elect Leader, George M. Leader Family Library and Archives, Box 10. Newspaper editorials in support of the governor-elect included the *Erie Daily Times, Harrisburg Patriot News, Kane Republican Lancaster New Era, Pottsville Republican, Philadelphia Inquirer, Pittsburgh Post-Gazette, Scranton Tribune,* and *Wilkes-Barre Times Leader*.

10. "The New Governor," *Lancaster New Era*, November 10, 1954, p. 14, "Public Backs Leader in Big Job Ahead," *Pottsville Republican*, November 10, 1954, p. 8.

94 / Chapter 3

11. Ruth Seltzer. "A Visit to the George M. Leaders," *Philadelphia Sunday Bulletin*, November 7, 1954, p. 7.
12. "Ike Proposes U.N. Seek Way to Stop War," and "7th Fleet Able for Action Commander Says," *Patriot*, January 20, 1955, p. 1.
13. "State's Economy to be his First Concern Leader says in his Inaugural Address," *Patriot*, January 19, 1955, p. 1.
14. "Text of Gov. Leader's Inaugural Address," *Patriot*. January 19, 1955, p. 5.
15. "York Father Proves Bi-Partishanship: Son Named George Leader," *Patriot*, January 19, 1955. p. 1.
16. "New Governor Celebrates 37th Year," *Patriot*, Tuesday January 18, 1955. p. 6.
17. "Leader Fills Dr. Haas' Post Temporarily, *Patriot*, January 20, 1955, p. 2
18. "Shapiro Launches Clean-Up," *Patriot*, January 21, 1955, p. 1.
19. "Revamp OK asked by Leader," *Patriot*, January 25, 1955, p. 1. Press Release, *Appointment of Commission on Governmental Affairs*. May 23, 1956, and *Commission on Governmental Reorganization: Recommendations Made to the Pennsylvania General Assembly*. March, 1957. Commonwealth of Pennsylvania Governor's Office, Harrisburg, PA. MG 207, George M. Leader Papers, MG 207, 9-0312, carton 7, folder 4/22, Pennsylvania State Archives, Harrisburg. Commonwealth of Pennsylvania Governor's Office, Harrisburg, PA
20. "Governor Leader Scans his Resignation as Squire," *Patriot*, January 14, 1955, p. 4.
21. "Ax is sharpened for State Payroll," *Patriot*, January 19, 1955, p. 6. Press Release, Commonwealth of Pennsylvania Governor's Office, Harrisburg, PA. George M. Leader Papers, MG 207, 9-0299, carton 10, folder 1/24, Pennsylvania State Archives, Harrisburg, PA.
22. "Tax Problem is Bi-Partisan, Leader Says: Seeks GOP Support," *Patriot*, January 18, 1955. p. 4
23. Unless indicated by footnote reference to commonwealth statutes reforms were implemented by Leader administration policy, executive order, or other administrative action.
24. Act 222 of 1955. Pennsylvania Fair Employment Practices Act. (November 30, 1955) *Laws of the General Assembly of the Commonwealth of Pennsylvania passed at the Session of 1955*. Volume I. Harrisburg, PA: Commonwealth of Pennsylvania, 1955, 744–56.
25. Act 255 of 1955. The Administrative Code as Amended. (December 14, 1955). *Laws of the General Assembly of the Commonwealth of Pennsylvania passed at the Session of 1955*. Volume I. Harrisburg, PA: Commonwealth of Pennsylvania, 1957, 853–65.

26. Act 455 of 1955. Anthracite Strip Mine Law as Amended. (April 4, 1956). *Laws of the General Assembly of the Commonwealth of Pennsylvania passed at the Session of 1955.* Volume I. Harrisburg, PA: Commonwealth of Pennsylvania, 1955, 1398–1401.

27. Act 537 of 1955. Pennsylvania Industrial Development Authority Act. (May 17, 1956). *Laws of the General Assembly of the Commonwealth of Pennsylvania passed at the Session of 1955.* Volume II. Harrisburg, PA: Commonwealth of Pennsylvania, 1955, 1609–21.

28. Act 429 of 1955. Public School Code as Amended. (March 29, 1956). *Laws of the General Assembly of the Commonwealth of Pennsylvania passed at the Session of 1955.* Volume II. Harrisburg, PA: Commonwealth of Pennsylvania, 1955, 1356–65.

29. Act 336 of 1955. The Insurance Company Law of 1921 as Amended. *Laws of the General Assembly of the Commonwealth of Pennsylvania passed at the Session of 1955.* (February 16, 1955). Volume I. Harrisburg, PA: Commonwealth of Pennsylvania, 1955, 1046–48.

30. Act 417 of 1957. Enlarging the Rights and Powers of Married Women as to Property and Contracts and repealing certain provisions. (July 17, 1957). *Laws of the General Assembly of the Commonwealth of Pennsylvania passed at the Session of 1957.* Harrisburg, PA: Commonwealth of Pennsylvania, 1957, 969.

31. Act 419 of 1957. An Act Relating to Comic Books, Magazines, and other publications as amended. July 17, 1957. *Laws of the General Assembly of the Commonwealth of Pennsylvania passed at the Session of 1957.* Harrisburg, PA: Commonwealth of Pennsylvania, 1957, 971.

32. Act 420 of 1957. An Act to Consolidate, Amend, and Revise the Penal Code of the Commonwealth of Pennsylvania. (July 17, 1957). *Laws of the General Assembly of the Commonwealth of Pennsylvania passed at the Session of 1957.* Harrisburg, PA: Commonwealth of Pennsylvania, 1957, 972–73.

33. Graeme Park, a colonial-era property, was acquired by the Commonwealth. Act 413 of 1957. *Laws of the General Assembly of the Commonwealth of Pennsylvania passed at the Session of 1957.* Harrisburg, PA: Commonwealth of Pennsylvania, 1957.

34. Act 375 of 1955. Chiropody Act. (March 2, 1956). *Laws of the General Assembly of the Commonwealth of Pennsylvania passed at the Session of 1955.* Harrisburg, PA: Commonwealth of Pennsylvania, 1955, 1206–11.

35. Act 396 of 1955. Dog Law of 1921 as amended. (March 15, 1956). *Laws of the General Assembly of the Commonwealth of Pennsylvania passed at the Session of 1955.* Harrisburg, PA: Commonwealth of Pennsylvania, 1955, 1290–1311.

36. Press Release, September 24, 1956. Commonwealth of Pennsylvania Governor's Office, Harrisburg, PA. George M. Leader Papers, MG 207, 9-0315, carton 8, folder 8/42, Pennsylvania State Archives, Harrisburg.

37. Cooper and Crary, 1982, 10.

38. Cooper and Crary, 10, 1982. See also, Reed Smith. State Government in Transition: Reforms of the Leader Administration, 1955-1959. (Philadelphia, PA: University of Pennsylvania Press, 1963).

39. George M. Leader, interview with by Kenneth C. Wolensky, April 17, 2009, Hershey, PA.

40. Henry Leader, interview with Kenneth C. Wolensky, May 7, 2009, York, PA.

41. George M. Leader, interview with Kenneth C. Wolensky, January 31, 2009, Hershey, PA.

42. *Pennsylvania Manual, 1988*. Renee Lamis. *The Realignment of Pennsylvania Politics Since 1960: Two-Party Competition in a Battleground State.* (University Park, PA: Penn State University Press, 2009).

43. *Report of the Achievements of the Leader Administration.* October 20, 1955. Commonwealth of Pennsylvania Governor's Office, Harrisburg, PA. George M. Leader Papers, MG 207, 9-0299, carton 1, folder 1/4, Pennsylvania State Archives, Harrisburg.

44. George M. Leader, interview with Kenneth C. Wolensky, January 31, 2009, and April 17, 2009, Hershey, PA.

45. "Industrial Development Plan of the Leader Administration." Commonwealth of Pennsylvania Governor's Office, Harrisburg, PA. George M. Leader Papers, MG 207, 9-0168 and 9-0168, cartons 19 and 20. Pennsylvania State Archives, Harrisburg.

46. Press Release, October 3, 1956. Commonwealth of Pennsylvania Governor's Office, Harrisburg, PA, MG 207, George M. Leader Papers, MG 207, 9-0315, carton 8, folder 42, Pennsylvania State Archives, Harrisburg. *Pennsylvania Industrial Development Advertising Program*, September 1956 to May 1957. Pennsylvania Department of Commonwealth, Bureau of Industrial Development, Harrisburg, PA. George M. Leader Papers, MG 207, 9-0169, container 20, folder 2, Pennsylvania State Archives, Harrisburg.

47. *Greater Pittsburgh*, January 1958, 27–38 that featured articles by Governor Leader, Secretary of Commerce William R. Davlin, and Secretary of Labor and Industry William L. Batt, Jr. George M. Leader Papers, MG 207, 9-0169, container 20, folder 2, Pennsylvania State Archives, Harrisburg.

48. George M. Leader, interview with Kenneth C. Wolensky, February 25, 2009, Hershey, PA; Wolensky, "Born a Leader," 2002.

49. *Address of the Honorable George M. Leader, Governor of the Commonwealth of Pennsylvania at the CIO Convention, March 16, 1956, Bellevue-Strat-*

ford Hotel, Philadelphia, Pennsylvania. George M. Leader Papers, MG 207, 9-0299, container 1, folder 1/42. State Archives, Harrisburg, PA.

50. Press Release, March 12, 1957. Commonwealth of Pennsylvania Governor's Office, Harrisburg, PA. George M. Leader Papers, MG 207, 9-0324, carton 11, folder 44, Pennsylvania State Archives, Harrisburg. George M. Leader and Elisabeth Myers, *Unlocking the Doors: Harry Shapiro and the Reforms of the Pennsylvania Mental Health System* (Harrisburg, PA: David A. Smith Printing, 2005). Ernest Morrison. *The City on the Hill: A History of the Harrisburg State Hospital*. (Self-published, 1992).

51. Henry Leader, interview with Kenneth C. Wolensky, May 7, 2009, York, PA.

52. George M. Leader, interview with Kenneth C. Wolensky, February 25 and August 28, 2009, Hershey, PA.

53. George M. Leader Papers, MG 207. 9-0185 through 9-0319. Pennsylvania State Archives, Harrisburg.

54. *Report of the Achievements of the Leader Administration*. October 20, 1955. Commonwealth of Pennsylvania Governor's Office, Harrisburg, PA. George M. Leader Papers, MG 207, 9-0309, carton 5, folder 5, Pennsylvania State Archives, Harrisburg.

55. George M. Leader, interview with Kenneth C. Wolensky, April 17, 2009, Hershey, PA.

56. Morrison (2000).

57. Press Release, September 24, 1956. Commonwealth of Pennsylvania Governor's Office, Harrisburg, PA. George M. Leader Papers, MG 207, 9-0312, carton 8, folder 42, Pennsylvania State Archives, Harrisburg.

58. George M. Leader, interview with Kenneth C. Wolensky, April 17, 2009.

59. "Ground is Broken at Gifford Pinchot State Park," *Sunday Patriot-News*, May 11, 1958, p. 1. One state park dedication, Glendale, Indiana County, proved amusing for both the governor and the media. Leader was charged with pushing a plunger in an ignition box to set off a dynamite charge to break ground. However, the dynamite would not fire on his first and second attempts. Engineers had to re-wire the charges and the governor tried again, successful the third time. "Governor Gets Two Duds Before Blast: Dedication of Glendale State Park," *Nanty-Glo Journal*, May 8, 1958, p. 7.

60. Char Miller. *Gifford Pinchot and the Making of Modern Environmentalism* (Washington, D.C.: Island Press, 2001); Harold Steen, ed. *The Conservation Diaries of Gifford Pinchot* (Durham, N.C.: The Forest History Society, 2001); and, Kenneth C. Wolensky. "He, On the Whole, Stood First: Pennsylvania's Gifford Pinchot," *Pennsylvania Heritage*, 30, no. 1. Winter, 2004, 20–27.

61. George M. Leader, Interview with Kenneth C. Wolensky, February 25 and August 28, 2009, Hershey, PA
62. Act 496 of 1955. The Motor Vehicle Code as amended. (April 20, 1956). *Laws of the General Assembly of the Commonwealth of Pennsylvania passed at the Session of 1955,* Harrisburg, PA: Commonwealth of Pennsylvania, 1955. 1502–3.
63. George M. Leader, interview with Kenneth C. Wolensky, August 28, 2009, Hershey, PA.
64. George M. Leader Papers, MG 207, 9-0150, carton 8-13. Pennsylvania State Archives, Harrisburg.
65. Report of the Achievements of the Leader Administration. October 20, 1955. George M. Leader Papers, MG 207, 9-0309, carton 5, folder 41, Pennsylvania State Archives, Harrisburg. Press Release, November 13, 1956. Eric L. Smith and Kenneth C. Wolensky, "A Novel Public Policy: Pennsylvania's Fair Employment Practices Act of 1955." *Pennsylvania History*, 69, no. 4, Fall, 2002, 489–523.
66. George M. Leader, interview with Kenneth C. Wolensky, August 28, 2009, Hershey, PA.
67. George M. Leader Papers, MG 207, 9-0318, cartons 11 and 12. Pennsylvania State Archives, Harrisburg.
68. Press Release, November 13, 1956. Commonwealth of Pennsylvania Governor's Office, Harrisburg, PA. George M. Leader Papers, MG 207, 9-0318, carton 9, folder 41, Pennsylvania State Archives, Harrisburg.
69. George M. Leader, interview with Kenneth C. Wolensky, April 17, 2009, Hershey, PA.
70. *Report of Achievements of the Leader Administration.* October 11, 1957. Commonwealth of Pennsylvania Governor's Office, Harrisburg, PA. George M. Leader Papers, MG 207, 9-0316, carton 49, folder 8, Pennsylvania State Archives, Harrisburg.
71. George M. Leader, interview with Kenneth C. Wolensky, April 17, 2009, Hershey, PA.
72. Veto of Act 5 of 1957. Liquor Code. (May 9, 1957). *Vetoes by the Governor of Bills Passed by the General Assembly of the Commonwealth of Pennsylvania Session of 1957.* Harrisburg, PA: Commonwealth of Pennsylvania, 1955, 11–13.
73. George M. Leader, interview with Kenneth C. Wolensky, April 17, 2009, Hershey, PA.
74. Letter to Senator Albert Gore from George M. Leader. March 25, 1955. Commonwealth of Pennsylvania Governor's Office, Harrisburg, PA. MG 207, George M. Leader Papers, 9-0189, carton 37, folder 8, Pennsylvania State Archives, Harrisburg.

75. *Internal Memo on Execution Statistics*. Camp Hill, PA: Pennsylvania Department of Corrections.
76. George M. Leader, interview with Kenneth C. Wolensky, January 31, 2009, and April 17, 2009, Hershey, PA.
77. Veto of Act 23 of 1957. The Pennsylvania Civil Procedural Support Law. (July 8, 1957) *Vetoes by the Governor of Bills Passed by the General Assembly of the Commonwealth of Pennsylvania Session of 1957*. Harrisburg, PA: Commonwealth of Pennsylvania, 1957, 51–53.
78. Act 417 of 1957.
79. Act 419 of 1957.
80. Act 420 of 1957.
81. *Address by the Honorable George M. Leader at the Final General Session of the Governor's Conference on Fitness*. November 7, 1958. Commonwealth of Pennsylvania Governor's Office, Harrisburg, PA. MG 207, George M. Leader Papers, MG 207, 9-0299, carton 1, folder 1/4, Pennsylvania State Archives, Harrisburg.
82. Press Release, November 13, 1956. Commonwealth of Pennsylvania Governor's Office, Harrisburg, PA. George M. Leader Papers, MG 207, 9-0318, carton 9, folder 9/4, Pennsylvania State Archives, Harrisburg. Also see, Smith, Eric L. and Kenneth C. Wolensky, "A Novel Public Policy: Pennsylvania's Fair Employment Practices Act of 1955." *Pennsylvania History*, 69, no. 4, Autumn 2002, 489–523.
83. George M. Leader, interview with Kenneth C. Wolensky, January 31, 2009, and April 17, 2009, Hershey, PA.
84. McCartney, Scott. ENIAC: *The Triumph and Tragedy of the World's First Computer*. London: Berkley Trade, 2001.
85. Veto of Act 19 of 1955. Pennsylvania Revenue Code as Amended. *Vetoes by the Governor of Bills Passed by the General Assembly of the Commonwealth of Pennsylvania passed at the Session of 1955*. (March 16, 1956). Harrisburg, PA: Commonwealth of Pennsylvania, 1955, 38–46.
86. George M. Leader, interview with Kenneth C. Wolensky, August 28, 2009, Hershey, PA.
87. Veto of Act 90 of 1957. An Act to provide for the Health and Safety of persons employed in and around Bituminous coal mines in Pennsylvania. (July 18, 1957), 201–4. *Vetoes by the Governor of Bills Passed by the General Assembly, Session of 1957*. Harrisburg, PA: Commonwealth of Pennsylvania, 1957.
88. George M. Leader, interview with Kenneth C. Wolensky, August 28, 2009. Hershey, PA.
89. *Final Message of George M. Leader, Governor of Pennsylvania, to the General Assembly of Pennsylvania, January 6, 1959 at Harrisburg*. George M. Leader Papers, MG 207, 9-0319, box 17, folder 17/23.

90. "George M. Leader – The Dedicated Liberal," by Paul Beers. *The Sunday Patriot-News*, August 23, 1964, p. B12.

91. "George M. Leader – The Dedicated Liberal," by Paul Beers.

92. "The Senate Race in Pennsylvania," *The Philadelphia Inquirer*, October 16, 1958, p. 14.

93. George M. Leader interview with Kenneth C. Wolensky, August 28, 2009, Hershey, PA.

94. Mary Jane Leader, interview with Kenneth C. Wolensky, June 29, 2009, Hershey, PA.

95. The Leaders were the only Pennsylvania first family with four children under the age of 14.

4

The 1958 U.S. Senate Campaign and Postgubernatorial Years

The inauguration of Democrat David Lawrence on January 20, 1959, was much like Leader's. It was very cold and windy that day in Harrisburg. Snow flurries fell and but the inaugural spirit wasn't dampened as several thousand were in attendance. Democrats, including Leader, were encouraged by the fact that Lawrence secured 2,204,852 votes compared to his opponent's 1,948,000 despite that registration remained in favor of the Republican Party with 2,897,307 registrants compared to 2,450,396 Democrats.[1]

Not long after the swearing-in the Leader family departed for home in York County. It is the tradition for the outgoing governor to politely yield to the new governor and quietly slip out of Harrisburg.[2] Leader reflects on his successor's election:

> GL:[3] The Democrats fussed around trying to find the right person to run and finally David Lawrence got in touch with me and said that he would like to run. Now back in those days it was pretty well established that a Catholic couldn't be elected governor and a Jew couldn't be elected governor and a woman couldn't be elected governor. It may or may not have been true. Later it turned out it wasn't true because we've had at least three Catholic governors and at least two Jewish governors. But we have yet to have the first lady governor, but I don't think that's too far off. Lawrence had been the Democratic National Committee man for years and he had been the Mayor of Pittsburgh and he had turned the city around from being perhaps the dirtiest city in America

because of the smoke from the steel mills, to what was later on rated as one of the most livable cities in America. So he had a great reputation, but he was a Catholic and he frankly was afraid that a Catholic couldn't win. It was interesting. I heard him say this with my own ears. He ran against a man from Reading by the name of Arthur McGonigle. Some of the people who weren't too well-informed thought, "Well, McGonigle sounds like an Irish-Catholic name, so we'll vote for Lawrence, he sounds like a Protestant." I think he (Lawrence) got a lot of votes from bigots who thought McGonigle was a Catholic and Lawrence was a Protestant. Well anyway, Lawrence won by a comfortable margin.

Leader didn't leave Harrisburg without one more political crusade, however. Only this time it had nothing to do with the governorship or having to yield it to Lawrence. Rather, it was on another political stage. In the spring of 1958 Leader announced then accepted his party's nomination to run for United States Senator from Pennsylvania against Hugh Scott, an eight-term incumbent Philadelphia congressman who was a favorite of the state's Republican stalwarts. U.S. Senator and former governor Edward Martin was retiring that year. To the GOP Scott was the natural heir. Though somewhat reluctant to reenter the political fray, Leader and the Democrats thought that Martin's seat could be turned around:

KW: In 1958 you were the Democratic Senatorial candidate.

GL: Yes, I was in that campaign in '58. I had thought I wanted to run for lieutenant governor in 1958 with Dave Lawrence to position myself to run for governor again at the end of the four years. Governors had a four-year limit. You couldn't have two consecutive four-year terms. My close associates said I had to be out of my mind to want to run for lieutenant governor but sometimes you must do the unexpected. If I had run as lieutenant governor I would have been elected and I could have positioned myself to run for governor again and get a second term under the old constitution of 1874. But they talked me out of that and I ran for the U.S. Senate. I was not anxious to go to Washington. My family was young and if you're in Washington from Pennsylvania you've got to come back here virtually every weekend and make speeches and travel around. It would have given me practically no time with my family. I really wasn't intrigued by the idea. I had served in state senate and legislative bodies are—unless you happen to be one of the four or five people that rise to the top—

you really feel fairly powerless. Legislative bodies have such a fragmentation of power and they're so influenced by the executive branch you really don't feel you're accomplishing much. I'm a doer. I'm an action-oriented person. I don't like to just talk about things. I like to talk about them and then do them. The "do" has to come pretty fast to make me happy and make me feel like my life is worthwhile and that I'm spending my life productively. That's why I wanted to run for lieutenant governor because I felt I could be more of a doer. I wasn't sure that would be the case being a U.S. Senator. I thought that the Democrats had a chance against Martin's legacy and Scott's campaign. If you don't believe in it you can't convey it to others. I thought we had a chance.

By mid-May, 1958, Leader had established his campaign, was raising some money.[4] From there, however, the campaign was an uphill struggle:

GL: My opponent, Hugh Scott, was a Congressman and was a servant of the Mellon organization in Pittsburgh and throughout Pennsylvania. When he was elected to the U.S. Senate he represented the special interests. The Mellons were giving $20,000 a year to his law firm in Philadelphia. Later on Gulf Oil began sending the money directly to Hugh Scott. He had a lot of money for his campaign. Scott was a Republican and he was able to go to Pittsburgh and get a lot of Democratic votes. So, he had Pittsburgh and Philadelphia in his column. He ran well in Philadelphia for a Republican. It was, by that time, a Democratic city. When a candidate has Philadelphia and Pittsburgh, Gulf Oil, and the Mellons in his column, he's pretty tough to defeat. That's what I faced despite the fact that I had served as governor for four years and had pretty good name recognition.

KW: What do you remember about the campaign?

GL: Well, I was burned out when I started the campaign. It was tough. I really had a hard time getting myself motivated for the campaign. I had run in '52 for State Treasurer and in '54 for governor and, in '56, I put a lot of time and effort into helping elect Joe Clark (1957–1969) to the U.S. Senate. So, in '58 I was running again for the U.S. Senate. I was running every two years and working hard for other candidates in the interim. It is very difficult to put yourself in a position to run for office every two years. It is just too hard, even in a congressional district, as opposed to the whole state. When I campaigned I went all out. I worked every day, all day into the night. I was young, I was strong, and I was in good health, thank goodness, but running every two years is just brutal. Oddly enough, after I lost for the Senate they wanted me to run for congressman for the York County area. I said, "Look, I have been in campaigns four straight times—every two years. I just can't do it."

The major issue, according to newspapers and the public, was the 1958 "Eisenhower recession" in which high unemployment continued to plague the commonwealth. Industrial areas—Wilkes-Barre, Altoona, Johnstown, Pittsburgh—had double-digit unemployment rates to say nothing of underemployment as some of these areas were experiencing what historians and social scientists later came to call deindustrialization (Pennsylvania was among the first states in nation to deindustrialize).[5] The *Harrisburg Patriot-News*, and other regional newspapers, reported on the severity of the Pennsylvania economic downturn on its front page just after the May primary election; a story that shared the front page story was another attention grabber in which FBI Director J. Edgar Hoover made it clear that "rock and roll poses severe threats to American youth" by encouraging drug use, promiscuity, and rebellion against authority and that the FBI was looking into whether rock-and-roll musicians were influenced by communists or, worse, were themselves communists. Pennsylvania's U.S. Senate candidates had other issues on which to focus, however. Both Leader and Hugh Scott made it clear that national, state, and local unemployment remained their major area of focus.

Scott touted his qualifications for the job and claimed that Pennsylvanians were fortunate to have a candidate with "16 years of experience as a federal representative while my opponent has had none at all." And, with such experience, jobs and the economy had been and would remain at the top of his list. He insisted that he would require any federal economic development legislation be "accompanied by cash" rather than empty political promises. (Federal economic development legislation was debated in Congress throughout most of the 1950s and resulted in the Flood-Douglas Area Redevelopment Act of 1961 that was signed by President Kennedy and provided tens of millions in job creation and economic development programs through the Office of Economic

Opportunity in the U.S. Department of Commerce. Funding was targeted at Appalachia and urban areas. The chief House sponsor was Congressman Daniel J. Flood of Pennsylvania's 11th district and U.S. Senator Paul Douglas of Illinois, both Democrats who leaned liberal on economic issues.) Moreover, Scott promised to vote against any federal tax increase to deal with the government's $12.2 billion deficit. To the contrary, he promised to push for federal tax cuts to promote for business and personal investment to stimulate the economy.[6] Government and the private sector had to work together to solve the economic problem, he said.

Leader, touting his record as governor of one of the largest states in the union, made it clear that his economic development program in PIDA had begun to chip away at unemployment and attracted many new industries. While it was not a complete panacea, PIDA had made measurable progress. He fully supported economic development programs at the federal level and expressed hesitation that businesses should benefit from substantial tax cuts and without ordinary citizens having their taxes reduced. Leader was fully confident that his experience as governor made him equally if not better qualified than Scott to be U.S. Senator. After all, Scott had never balanced a budget, never exercised executive authority, and had had easy reelections to Congress in which Leader said he often skirted the issues of concern to ordinary people.

U.S. Senators work on a national and world stage. Thus, Pennsylvania's issues aren't their only focus. Defense, trade, and labor racketeering (a major issue in the 1950s) had to be addressed as well. On defense, Leader supported a strong domestic defense in light of the Soviet threat and made it clear that "America shouldn't be pushed around." However, he cautioned against U.S. financial support for militarism in foreign nations, pointing out that U.S. policy should demand clear results in terms of those nations building their own military infrastructure as the United States "could not go it alone."[7]

On trade, Leader favored reciprocal agreements with friendly nations and insisted that trade must be balanced. He did not want the United States to have a trade deficit, wanted trade to build up the domestic economy and that of trading partners and argued that import and export tariffs had to be equitable. On the problem of labor racketeering—perhaps best epitomized by Robert F. Kennedy's relentless pursuit of by James R. Hoffa and the International

Brotherhood of Teamsters—Leader, too, had strong views. He made it clear that he supported Kennedy-sponsored legislation to make certain financial transactions within labor unions illegal, require additional reporting to the U.S. Department of Labor on any union-related financial investments especially in real estate and pension funds, and argued that the absolute power exercised by Hoffa and Dave Beck of the AFL-CIO paved the way for corruption.[8]

Scott's views weren't entirely dissimilar. On labor he supported "a bill which would put under control, discipline, and punish any labor official who takes that which is not his from another man . . . such as those who prey on or embezzle from dues payers." He was less concerned should organized labor offer any support for him. Rooting out the Hoffas was far more important than votes. He was adamant that Leader stop telling the public that Scott balked when it came to real support for Dan Flood's Area Redevelopment Act. He supported federal economic development aid but made it clear that money must accompany the legislation and that no money line the pockets of elected and appointed officials. On trade Scott said that it should be fair and balanced and advocated federal support (tax and otherwise) for American companies who engaged in it. Finally, Scott supported a strong national defense and thought, too, that U.S. foreign and military policy should especially support nations threatened by communists.[9]

Both Leader and Scott campaigned vigorously and used the media for newspaper and television advertising. Despite his statewide name recognition and tough campaigning, Leader never quite pulled ahead in polling; he usually trailed by several points at least. On election day in early November, Scott was victorious with 2.02 million votes. Leader was happy that he campaigned as well as Scott despite his loss with 1.92 million votes.[10] He was also tired. Scott took office in early January as Governor and Mary Jane Leader and their children prepared to depart Harrisburg as Governor-elect David Lawrence assumed the reins of state government. Besides the election and inauguration, another story continued to dominate headlines in the late fall and early winter of 1958–1959. Cuba's new dictator, Fidel Castro, and his rebels had seized control of Havana and the entire nation, ousted President Battista, forced organized crime out of the casino and related businesses, and promised substantial (and severe) changes to policies, economics, and social conditions of the tiny island nation.[11] The U.S. government wasn't completely surprised by Castro's overthrow as intelligence forces indicated its imminence.

Thus ended George Leader's political career. He would be considered for statewide office on several occasions though he never seriously considered it again. For example, in 1982 Leader was encouraged by the state Democratic Party to take on incumbent governor Dick Thornburgh. He turned it down.[12] Thornburgh narrowly won against attorney Allen Ertel by 100,000 out of nearly four million votes cast. The rapidly deindustrializing Pennsylvania economy made Thornburgh, a Republican, less popular that in 1978 when he defeated fellow Pittsburgher Pete Flaherty by a slightly more comfortable margin of 250,000 votes.[13]

Though he exited from the public stage Leader remained an important figure in state politics. In one of his better-known public speeches shortly after turning down the 1980s gubernatorial offer Leader publicly criticized the idea that most people—except those in ill health or who faced no other choice—should retire. Work meant happiness and something to live for, he told a Harrisburg group of senior citizens at a luncheon honoring the accomplishments of a select group of their peers. Retirement for males was simply a recipe for "widow making" he said. People in their senior years should remain active with their families, work, and community, they should travel, and they should simply enjoy life. Some seniors at the luncheon were, apparently, taken aback by the vehemence of Leader's views, especially the comment about widow-making.[14] Perhaps Leader was hinting that, at the age of 64, he had no intention of ever retiring himself nor did he have any intention of making Mary Jane a widow.

Governor Leader talks about his departure from public office and his pursuit of other opportunities:

KW: In 1958 you departed elected office in Pennsylvania forever.

GL: Well, I didn't necessarily plan it that way but that's how it worked out. Following the U.S. Senate race, in the early 1960s I was offered the opportunity to run for Congress representing York and parts of Adams counties. I did want to stay in politics but it wasn't the time. I was burned out. So, I didn't run and, as it turned out, bowed out of politics for good.

KW: You were considered for high-level positions in the Kennedy administration when he was elected in 1960.

GL: I had interest in the Department of Health, Education, and Welfare (HEW). Senator Joe Clark knew I had interest and pushed for me to secure a position. Though he knew my interest in HEW he set up an interview for me with Morris Udall, who was Kennedy's Secretary of the Interior. The interview was on the day of Kennedy's inauguration in January 1961. So, the day of the inauguration I got as far as the outskirts of Washington and the snow and cold were so bad that I turned around and came back home. Moreover, I didn't particularly want to be in that field. Being one of Secretary Udall's Deputy Secretaries didn't appeal to me. In those days, Deputy Secretaries earned $15,000 a year. There's no way that I could have supported my family and lived in Washington. I couldn't commute to Washington every day. So, I was discouraged and I turned around and came back home and cancelled the appointment. I watched the inauguration on the television. Outside there was about twelve inches of snow but they cleared Washington and they had a tremendous inauguration. Another opportunity that I had was to run the Small Business Administration under President Johnson. I was interviewed by the administration officials. As it turned out, I didn't want to do that either. I knew how political that agency was and I knew how much pressure Congressmen and Senators could put on that agency. When you are dealing with money, government money, you can be pressured by the political forces and put yourself in great jeopardy if someone isn't satisfied. The Small Business Administration is a political hot spot. I knew some of the kinds of people that were promoting small business loans here in Pennsylvania and they were the kind of people that would do anything to make a dollar.

KW: You didn't want to be part of that?

GL: I didn't want to be part of that because I didn't want to put myself in that kind of jeopardy. There was a lot of dishonesty involved and I wasn't cut out for that.

KW: Did you consider any other opportunities?

GL: I was asked of my interest in serving as president of West Chester State College. I turned that down. But the best opportunity I ever had was when Judge Fullum, a federal judge who presided over the Penn Central Railroad in bankruptcy, asked me to be chairman of its Board of Trustees in bankruptcy. Judge Fullum was from Montgomery County and he was a fine man. I would have been very happy to work with him as a person. He had run for the State Senate when I ran for governor in '54, but he lost. Anyway, he called me, said he'd like me to be his man for the chair of the board of trustees. He trusted me and knew I'd be honest with him. I didn't take it. I said, "How long do I have to decide?" He said, "24 hours." I said, "What does it pay?" He said, "Oh, six figures." I was making $25,000—that was four times what I was earning. So, that night I talked to the five people closest to me—my wife, my brother, my political advisor, and two others. All of them said, "take it." I'll never forget my partner in the nursing home business, Phil Berman. Phil said, "You'll be invited to every cocktail party in New York." I thought, that's a good reason not to take it. I didn't tell the judge that, because I didn't want to hurt his feelings, because he was being nice. To be invited to every cocktail in New York City, I would give $1,000 a night *not* to have to go to a cocktail party in New York City! It isn't my style. I don't fit in to the cocktail crowd; never did. The next day I was driving to one of our facilities in Williamsport and I stopped in a gas station with one of those telephone booths outside. I called the judge and I said, "Judge, I'm sorry. I am obligated to stay and take care of my nursing home business and meet the obligations I have." I really liked what I was doing. I thought I was doing something for mankind. I would have had to work 12 or 14 hours a day, six and seven days a week, because the Penn Central had already been a mess. I had to learn everything from square one. I was not a transportation person. I wasn't bringing a lot along except my integrity. So, I turned it down. But that was probably the best job offer. By that time I was starting to get into the long-term care field and we had a company with 12 million dollars' worth of borrowed money. I don't think my bankers would look too favorably on working somewhere else! Later, I was asked by the powers that be, including Governor Lawrence, to run for governor again, and I probably would have won. Our little company was in debt. We had three nursing and rehabilitation homes. We were just really learning the nursing home business in those days and getting more proficient at it. We were doing a better job than average. I loved what I was doing and my wife was helping me—we were a team. And I think after we got to know the ropes, we got to do a pretty good job. It was called Leader Nursing and Rehabilitation Center(s).

KW: Governor, what was it like for you to leave the governor's office and to return to being a private citizen?

GL: Well, we lived in a lovely house with a big mortgage and my total income the first six months was 150 dollars! I noticed when Governor Thornburgh decided to run for U.S. Senate in the early 1990s his Pittsburgh law firm gave him something like $384,000 a year salary. I was not a lawyer and I said I didn't learn to steal young enough because I didn't have much money when I left office! We had a nice farm and I had agreed to put $12,000 into doing some remodeling for the house. When the bills came in they were $22,000 and I didn't have $22,000. It took me about two years to pay that off because before long I was earning about $20,000 a year. I didn't have a lot of money and whatever we had was based on the fact that the G.I. Bill of Rights permitted you to buy or borrow up to 100 percent on property. So I had bought a poultry farm for $25,000 and borrowed about $25,000. My net worth was about $3,500. That became my working capital but in a year or so that was pretty well gone and I needed more. And then my father endorsed a note for me for $2,500 and that tided me over until we got operating comfortably into the black. Whatever I have today is based on that $25,000 mortgage that I got under the G.I. Bill of Rights. When Tom Brokaw wrote about "the greatest generation" there were the greatest for two reasons. One, they paid for higher education for all of us GIs if we wanted it. I already had a college education, so I didn't go back. Second, the government financed real estate for us, up to 100 percent for GIs. That helped me to get started. Then I moved in to mortgage banking.

KW: Why did you get into mortgage banking?

GL: I was impressed with our Pennsylvania Industrial Development Authority, that was based on first mortgages from a lending institution, second mortgages from the local industrial development authority, and third mortgages from the state. I thought mortgaging is a wonderful thing and I wanted to know more about it. I got into mortgage banking and I got a good education. Part of our success in long-term care was based on my knowledge of mortgages because when you go into an industry like long-term care, where you have major investments in real estate, you've got to figure out how to finance it. So, for the first two years of mortgage banking I worked from home in York County. Then we had to move to Philadelphia for career purposes and, having a blind son, our children's education, of course, took a very high priority. When I had been a student at Penn every Thursday night the school had a dinner meeting and they would bring in an public office holder in different areas; school board, a township or borough. Many times professionals came from Lower Merion Township. So when we decided to move to the Philadelphia area for my job as a mortgage banker Mary Jane and I decided to look into Lower Merion Township. Mary Jane called the superintendent of schools in Lower Merion Township and set up an appointment. We got into our car and drove down there and we met with the superintendent. He had one of his assistant superintendents with him for the meeting. He was a very nice man. A well-qualified man. We asked him, "Would you take a blind student?" He said, "Well if he can do the work." We said, "He's a straight A student everywhere he's ever been." He said, "Well we graduated a blind student from high school last year, so that would be fine." So we set up to go Lower Merion Township. We found a house, a lovely four-bedroom house that we could rent, and we moved down there and put our children in the Lower Merion schools. It worked out beautifully. The amazing thing about the Lower Merion school is the fact that they not only put their 90-some percent of their children in colleges or universities, but if you look over the list, they put an awful lot of them in Ivy League schools and comparable, high-quality places. And our children all had the chance to go to Ivy League schools when they graduated from Lower Merion. We moved into a town called Gladwyne and our house was very close to the elementary school, and of course they had to be bused to the middle school and the high school. We lived down there in that area for about 23 years. Our children went through the school system and went on to college before we left there.

KW: How does a York County farmer fit in with the Philadelphia main line and mortgage banking?

GL: Well, that's a very interesting question. It wasn't easy. Gladwyne was developed for the people who provided service to the people in Bryn Mawr, a much more exclusive area. In Gladwyne lived the maids, the groundskeepers, and others. It was nice and had some very beautiful areas. Bryn Mawr, of course, was for the upper class. There were two Presbyterian churches, the big Presbyterian church of Bryn Mawr and a small Presbyterian church in Gladwyne that we joined. Gladwyne was surrounded by huge houses and there were a lot of small houses there that were reasonably priced and reasonable to rent. It's a nice little town, lovely little town. I am not sure that we ever fit into the Main Line but we were comfortable in Gladwyne. Frankly, it didn't matter if we fit in or not. Well, we were introduced to Gladwyne by the superintendent of schools. We said, "where should we live—what would you recommend?" He said, "Well you ought to go to Gladwyne. We've got a wonderful elementary school over there, and your children will do well." The principal was a saint. He helped to serve milkshakes to the children every day and he saw to it that the children that came from poor homes and that might need the nourishment would get a second milkshake. That's the kind of man he was. Someone said, "If you love children, and the children love you, learning is almost sure to take place." Learning took place in the Gladwyne Elementary School because of that man.

On mortgage banking, it was interesting. I learned a great deal but knew it wasn't where I wanted to spend the rest of my life. I began looking into where I might have some business prospects and I learned more about long-term care in the mortgage banking business. That's were I decided to concentrate my efforts.

KW: When did you first get the idea to go into long-term care?

GL: I think, probably, when I was visiting the mental hospitals as governor. I visited almost every one of the mental hospitals. Every superintendent, or the person that took us through, had a big key ring—maybe six or eight inches in diameter—full of keys. Every time we went through another set of doors, he unlocked it with a different key. Then Harry Shapiro and I went over to England, to Worlingham Park, which is an hour or two drive out of London. There was a Doctor Reese who ran a very advanced mental hospital there. Harry told me I should visit there one day to see how advanced patient treatment was compared to the United States. We went to visit in 1957. Well, the front gate was open. We just went through the gate. The patients were playing cricket in uniform. I went into a room with a group of men and all of them were dressed in business suits and vests, some of them with chains and watches. I learned afterwards that those were the most challenging mental health patients and I was in there without any staff member. These gentlemen were just wonderful. I said to Dr. Reese, "How do you do this?" He said he tried to run a humane institution and tried to work with the patients, give them self-worth and a sense of being human. Here in Pennsylvania, and we had 40,000 plus people in our mental hospitals when I came on the scene. They couldn't adjust to their environment, community, job, family, or life in general so they were "put away" as the term went. England, on the other hand, at least gave people some hope. Well, that influenced me in terms of long-term care. I thought, "if England can do that for their mental patients, we can help the elderly and the sick live in dignity here in the United States." That was my philosophy when I went into long-term care. A friend of mine suggested that I go into long-term care. I said to Mr. Martin, my boss at the mortgage company, "I'd like to go into the long-term care field but I don't think I ever saw a nursing home in Pennsylvania that I want to put my name on." He said, "Well, you would like the ones on the west coast. I have a file on them and I'll send it to you." He did. I picked up the phone and called the president of the company out there and I made an appointment to go to California there and spend several days with them.

KW: What was the name of the company?

GL: Hill Haven. The president was Fred Diamond. He took me along with him on his routes to go see the different homes on the west coast. This was in '59 or '60. I went out there and I was amazed. You could eat off the floor in the nursing homes. His staff wore white uniforms. The place was spotless, odor-free. And that's when I was really sure I should be in long-term care and we should be doing this sort of thing in Pennsylvania. We needed and deserved that quality in Pennsylvania.

KW: How did you put the business together?

GL: It wasn't easy because I didn't have the money to get started. Every new business needs some capital because in the early years you're bound to lose money. Nobody can start a new business and make money the first month, the first day, the first year. You'll be lucky if you're making money by the third or fourth year. Our first facility was in '63 in Camp Hill. I got my inspiration—from Hill Haven. We started out with one, of course, and in a relatively short time we had three. One was in Camp Hill, one was in Yeadon next to Lansdowne, a suburb of Philadelphia that had been a Quaker community originally. The third one was in the Cheltenham area of Philadelphia. We had three and we were losing money in all of them. We were 120 days in arrears in the payment of our bills. My partner was running them. He was good at raising money and I wasn't. I'm not good at raising money. He was also in charge of operations but he was a lousy operator. We were 120 days in arrears and vendors said, "You're going to have to pay cash, or we're not going to deliver it to you." So I said, "Chuck, I can't sleep at night on this. Either you buy me out, or I'll buy you out." I didn't want to be a party to a failure if I could help it. So he sold out to me. Mary Jane and I took it over and we went to my banker and borrowed money. Mary Jane called the vendors and said, "We'll bring the payables down to 30 days in another week or two, as soon as we get this loan through our bank." The money wasn't loaned to the company—I bought more stock in the company with that money, because we needed more capital. Pretty soon we had it down to 60 days and we worked on it, and it wasn't long till we had it down to 30 days. Then the vendors knew we were as good as our word and we didn't have trouble getting deliveries after that. But it took us three or four years until we got in the black substantially. Then I went over to New York and I was able to get an underwriting for a million dollars. We netted about a million fifty thousand. It was with that money we started expanding and in ten or twelve years we sold that company.

KW: That was Leader Nursing and Rehabilitation Centers. What year did you sell that?

GL: 1981. And we started Country Meadows in '82.

KW: How was Leader Nursing and Rehabilitation Centers different from the other nursing homes in Pennsylvania?

GL: Well, there were a few nursing homes that had good rehab programs. But most of them didn't. It took me a couple years to provide the equipment and staff. We didn't just change the name to rehabilitation. We actually put the programs in and then changed the name to Leader Nursing and Rehabilitation Centers. And from that point on, we did pretty well because we were ahead of the field.

KW: Your focus wasn't on warehousing people.

GL: No, it wasn't. I wanted to be proud of what we did. It's hard to believe, but back in those days if you said you were in the nursing home field there was a stigma attached to it. A lot of people in that field didn't like to talk about it. The field had not been dominated by a lot of dedicated people. I like to believe Mary Jane and I were different. We worked very hard and we took very small salaries. I can remember when Mary Jane was taking a $700 salary a month and we were paying someone $550 a month for a housekeeper to come in to fix meals for the children, because she didn't get home in time. So, until we paid the tax and all, it was a losing deal. We were always trying to build something. We were planners. We always worked for the long term, never for the short-term quick dollar.

Now, the children were all in public schools at that time. Later, Michael went to Haverford. Fred went to Swarthmore. He was admitted to Princeton, but he chose to go to Swarthmore. We had a trainer to familiarize Fred with the campus. The trainer made a clever map of the campus using Scotch tape and a string so that Fred could feel on the map and follow the string to walk around campus. Swarthmore was very good for him. Jane went to Lafayette. David was admitted to Harvard and Princeton, but chose Princeton. The kids all had good opportunities to go to first-class schools. Years ago the Lower Merion High School was chosen among the 25 best preparatory schools in the United States along with Exeter Academy and all the good ones. Lower Merion prepared our kids well for higher education.

KW: While you were in the nursing home business in the late 60s and the 1970s—what's your role, if any at all, in politics, in the state Democratic Party?

GL: I tried to run for National Democratic Committeeman, but I lost. They elected Joe Barr, the mayor of Pittsburgh at that time. They wanted to keep it in Pittsburgh, it wasn't anything against me personally, but Dave Lawrence had been a National Committeeman for years and he was the mayor of Pittsburgh before he was governor and they elected Joe Barr. I went to all the national conventions up until the time I left the governorship and then I discontinued going all the time. I was always a delegate when I went. In the very beginning in '52 I was an alternate delegate, but always after that I was a full-fledged delegate. As I said, in the early 80s the Democrats approached me to consider running for governor. I turned it down. I was simply too involved in my business ventures. Had I not been so involved, I would have run and, probably, would have won. Allen Ertel did well against Dick Thornburgh that year. He came very close to beating Thornburgh.

Maybe I could have beaten him? Remember, we were in the midst of a very severe "Reagan recession." Pennsylvania had lost tens of thousands of jobs. Steel mills and plants closed, laying off many skilled workers. It was a real shame. I never thought I'd live long enough to see that, especially Pennsylvania to lose its steel industry! Well, maybe I could have won that year but might have gotten frustrated because governors are limited in what they can do. They can work to rebuild the state economy like we did with PIDA. But the early 80s were very difficult years. Reagan and the Republicans weren't too popular in Pennsylvania when the severity of that recession hit. Then Reagan beat Mondale by a huge landslide in 1984. Pennsylvania went solidly Reagan. I never understood why because an industrial state like Pennsylvania suffered a great deal from Reagan's careless free-market philosophy. I don't know how smart or qualified he was to be President. But, apparently, he had popular appeal. In 1984 I supported Walter Mondale but knew his chances of winning were slim.

KW: In long-term care you soon had assistance from your son, Michael.

GL: Yes. Michael, my alter-ego, had graduated law school and was working in a very interesting job in Washington, D.C. He was involved in the movement to make Washington, D.C. an independent city. Eventually that happened. But he decided, while he was there, he said, "I'm going to go to law school." I said, "Well, Michael why don't you come home? Your mother and I are overloaded with the responsibility for running Country Meadows." He said, "Nope. I've made up my mind." He said, "I've got the money saved up and I'm going to go to law school." So he did. Then he came with us out of law school, first as our in-house counsel and then as the executive vice president, and, later, president. He's done a wonderful job. And I told him I would step out when I reached the age of 80, and he could become CEO. Not only did he get the title, but I transferred my voting shares over to him, so he controls 52 percent of the voting shares of the company, which belongs to my children. And my new company, Providence Place, belongs to my grandchildren already. They don't know it, but they have the voting rights to half of it. My partner, Jesse Achenbach, has 50 percent. He's the president of the company and I'm CEO. He's been a great partner.

KW: How did you incorporate your life philosophies into your business ventures?

GL: Well, I like new ideas. I like improving people's quality of life. I am very happy with that. Even now, I'm 91, and I think about how I can do a better job in my company every day. Every hour of every day. I was watching television about two weeks ago and I saw them using exercise to stimulate Parkinson's patients. There are a number of those diseases today that cause brain damage including Parkinson's, Alzheimer's, Multiple Sclerosis, and so forth. Well, on this TV show they did an experiment with chimpanzees. They had one group that exercised and one group, the control group, that didn't exercise. Then they did CAT scans on the brains after a given period of time. The damage to the brain of those that exercised was less than the size of an egg. The damage in the size of the brain that didn't exercise was bigger than a baseball. Now those chimpanzees—if it works on them—it probably would work on people. Then they showed how they had a belt to put around people so they could put them on a treadmill and exercise and chains would keep them from falling down if they tripped. So, I began to think on that subject, and I began to get on the phone and call people that are knowledgeable. Well, the result was that at Providence Place we are installing exercise equipment that can help those with dementia to improve their quality of life. With diseases like Parkinson's and Alzheimer's and Multiple Sclerosis, you've got to stimulate the brain and the body and the spirit. We have three religious services per week for our people in that section. Three half-hour sessions—because their capacity to stay focused is not as long as it could be sometimes. Now there are some drugs, and we use some of the drugs, but the drugs are not nearly as effective yet as we'd like them to be. They're helpful, but not totally. I'm so excited about what we're doing for dementia patients. I like to believe we're in the cutting edge of new ideas. And if we do a great job, then our competitors have to do a better job, too. On another note, Providence Place has $28 million dollars' worth of debt. Country Meadows has something over $100 million worth of debt. Now, we're operating in the black. We're meeting all of our obligations. We have sufficient working capital. We have good bankability and credit so we can afford to try new technology to improve quality of life. Anyway, after the governorship I had thought I wanted to get back into politics, maybe. But mortgage banking and long-term care exposed me to a whole new way of thinking. See, I like to apply what I learn from experience, from academics, from expertise, and from watching others. These fields helped me tremendously to do just that. And, I like to think that me and my family are improving peoples' lives and making their final years on this Earth as happy as possible.

I am very happy about that. I am very happy about that.

Notes

1. *Pennsylvania Manual*, Volume 105, 1986.
2. "Governorship Ends; Lawrence's Career Started at Age 14," *The Patriot*, January 19, 1959, p. 6.
3. George M. Leader, interview with Kenneth C. Wolensky, March 26, 2009, Hershey, PA.
4. "DEMS: Harrisburg Rally Will End Drive," *Sunday Patriot-News*, May 11, 1958, p. 9.
5. "Recession Seen as Top Issue," *Sunday Patriot-News*, May 11, 1958, p. 10. "FBI Chief raps Rock-n-Roll as Corrupting for Youths," *Sunday Patriot-News*, May 11, 1958, p. 10.
6. "Press Conference with the U.S. Senatorial Candidates," *Patriot-News*. October 19, 1958, pp. 4–12.
7. "Press Conference with the U.S. Senatorial Candidates"
8. "Press Conference with the U.S. Senatorial Candidates."
9. "Press Conference with the U.S. Senatorial Candidates."
10. *Pennsylvania Manual*, December, 1991, volume 110, p. 676.
11. "Havana Welcomes Rebel Hero Castro with Big Ovation," *The Patriot*, January 9, 1959, p. 1.
12. "Democrats Weigh Leader for Governor," *Reading Eagle*, November 5, 1981, p. 1
13. *Pennsylvania Manual*, December, 1991, volume 110, pp. 674–75.
14. "Help for Older Workers: Leader Lashes Out at Retirement as 'Widow Maker,'" *The Patriot*, May 4, 1984, p. 9.

Leader children Mary, Paul, Guy Alvin Jr., and George, ca. 1922. Courtesy of the Leader Library and Archives, Dover, York County, PA.

The Leader boys on their York County farm, ca. 1933. Left to right: Henry, Guy Alvin, Jr., George, and Paul. Courtesy of the Leader Library and Archives, Dover, York County, PA.

Navy Ensign George M. Leader, 1942. Courtesy of the Leader Library and Archives, Dover, York County, PA.

Senator Leader campaigns for governor, Gettysburg, Fall, 1954. Courtesy of the Leader Library and Archives, Dover, York County, PA.

Governor Leader is sworn in to office, January 18, 1954. Outgoing governor John Fine is on left. Chief Justice Charles Alvin Jones administers the oath. Behind Leader and Jones is Secretary of the Commonwealth Henry Harner. To the right is Guy Leader, Sr. and Mary Jane Leader. Courtesy of the Leader Library and Archives, Dover, York County, PA.

The Commonwealth's second youngest chief executive—37 years old—delivers his inaugural address as his father, wife, and son Michael look on. State Capitol, Harrisburg. Courtesy of the Leader Library and Archives, Dover, York County, PA.

George and Mary Jane at the inaugural ball, Zembo Mosque, Harrisburg. Courtesy of the Leader Library and Archives, Dover, York County, PA.

George and Mary Jane with children Frederick, Michael, David, and Jane, Executive Mansion, Harrisburg. Leader was Pennsylvania's only governor who had four young children during his term. Courtesy of the Leader Library and Archives, Dover, York County, PA.

Governor Leader signs Pennsylvania's first civil rights law, the Fair Employment Practices Act, 1956, Governor's Reception Room, State Capitol, Harrisburg. Courtesy of the Leader Library and Archives, Dover, York County, PA.

Leader tours a Commonwealth mental hospital in an effort to reform treatment. Commonwealth welfare secretary Harry Shapiro is behind Leader with other hospital officials. Leader's dissatisfaction with what he finds is apparent. 1955. Courtesy of the Leader Library and Archives, Dover, York County, PA.

The governor points to conditions in a state mental hospital latrine. Courtesy of the Leader Library and Archives, Dover, York County, PA.

A female mental hospital patient in solitary confinement. Courtesy of the Leader Library and Archives, Dover, York County, PA.

Leader with Democratic presidential nominee Adlai Stevenson, Governor's Reception Room, State Capitol, Harrisburg, 1956. Leader was considered by Stevenson to be his vice presidential nominee. Courtesy of the Leader Library and Archives, Dover, York County, PA.

Leader with Harry Truman on a get-out-the-vote for Adlai Stevenson campaign stop, Harrisburg, 1956. Courtesy of the Leader Library and Archives, Dover, York County, PA.

Governor, Mary Jane, and Michael with a state police escort tour a town in Northeastern Pennsylvania. Courtesy of the Leader Library and Archives, Dover, York County, PA.

Court of Common Pleas Judge Anne Alperin administers the oath of office to Genevieve Blatt, Pennsylvania's first female cabinet secretary, Secretary of Internal Affairs. Blatt and Leader were close political allies. Courtesy of the Leader Library and Archives, Dover, York County, PA.

George and Mary Jane Leader and Leader children and spouses, ca. 1995. Left to right: Governor Leader, daughter Jane and her husband Ted Janeczek, Mary Jane, daughter-in-law Karen and son Michael, son Fred and daughter-in-law Anne. Not in the photo is son David. Courtesy of the Leader family private collection.

The Governor and Mary Jane with children David, Jane, and Michael at the Leader farm near Hershey, Pennsylvania. Courtesy of the Leader family private collection.

5

Wellness, Faith, and Family

Wellness and Spirituality

Among the characteristics that have defined Governor Leader's eclectic life has been a commitment to certain spiritual and humanistic principles. The same is true for Mary Jane Leader. These principles have served him personally and in politics, family life, business, and in advocacy on social and political issues (for more on the latter subject see chapter 6). Mary Jane was usually somewhat reserved in talking about such matters. Her husband, however, is never reticent to share his principles, which are mainly centered in wellness and positive thinking. Governor Leader explains.

> KW: Governor, in the many years I've known you it is clear that you subscribe and live according to certain spiritual and humanistic principles. Let's start out with wellness. You have, for a long time, believed and practiced wellness. Why?
>
> GL:[1] The greatest impact of my life with regard to wellness is Greg Anderson and his speaking and his writing.[2] Greg was stricken with lung cancer in his early 30s. Greg had been a cigarette smoker, a heavy smoker. He already had one lung removed and thought he was in the clear. But then the remaining lung was diagnosed with cancer. He also had a large oozing growth on his neck and his oncologist told him to get his things in order because, if he was lucky, he had about 30 days to live. Lung cancer

is very deadly. I think that the long-term survival rate is about 5 percent. Well, in Greg's case, he was told he was going to die 28 years ago. But, that wasn't the end of his story.

After hearing the prognosis Greg was discharged from the hospital, went home and was sitting in his living room preparing to die. His little daughter, about a year and a half old, was sitting on the floor and playing, and his wife, between the tears, was trying to prepare the evening meal. He said, "Lord, I don't want to die. I want to live to see that little girl grow up, and I want to go to her wedding, and I want to see my grandchildren." He was determined to find a way to alter his prognosis that his doctor had made when he said he had 30 days to live. He began exploring what was available, and there was a doctor in Texas. His name was O. Carl Simonton and he was a psychiatrist who had dealt with patients who were told that they had a short time to live. Greg was on the staff of Dr. Robert Schuller's Crystal Cathedral Church in Garden Grove, California, where the "Hour of Power" originates. Dr. Schuller knew about this man in Texas and referred Greg to him. Greg called the physician and asked "What's the difference in your patients between the ones who live and the ones who die?" He said, "Well, I can't really answer that question. But if you really want to find out I'll give you their names and addresses and you can inquire of them." Well, when you have 30 days to live and you get advice from an outstanding psychiatrist you tend to follow that advice. You do something about it. So, Greg called on some of them in the Orange County area where Garden Grove is located. His main research question was to see what the difference was between patients who lived and patients who died. He found fourteen items. But there were three that prevailed almost entirely through his research. First, to survive you've got to have positive beliefs and positive attitudes. Second, you've got to practice forgiveness. I think forgiveness is something a lot of us Christians tend to overlook. We're not as good on forgiveness. We forget that the Lord's Prayer says "Forgive us as we forgive others." Third was unconditional, nonjudgmental love for yourself and others. The amazing thing is how all of these values relate to the teachings of many religions, especially Christianity and how close these very practical observations of people who thought they were going to die in a short time, how close they were to what Jesus taught. If Christianity can take those three principles to heart the billion or so Christians in the world could change the whole world. Well, Greg Anderson started working on forgiveness. He went to see one man with whom he had a terrible quarrel on budgetary matters at Crystal Cathedral. Greg had had a terrible falling out with the treasurer whose first name was Ollie. Apparently Greg wanted more money for his program than the treasurer was willing to put in the budget. Ollie became very sick as well. It turned out that man was ill and was dying of cancer. Greg says it's the hardest thing he ever did, but he got in his car and went to that man's home. He sat down on the bed with this man and he said, "I've been meaning to come to you and ask for your forgiveness." Greg was there to ask this man's forgiveness. They forgave each other. And I don't know what the outcome was for the treasurer but I know that was one of the turning points in Greg's life. I've been so impressed with positive attitudes, forgiveness, and unconditional love and what it has to do with the healing process, both mentally and physically, and, of course, spiritually. If we can forgive I think we can heal ourselves psychologically and maybe even cure ourselves of deadly diseases like cancer. Greg is alive and thriving today largely as a result of practicing the principles he learned from those who were long-term survivors of cancer.

KW: How did you find out about Greg Anderson?

GL: One of my principal charities had been The Institute for Successful Church Leadership at Dr. Schuller's church. That's a program Dr. Schuller of the Crystal Cathedral ran for 25 years or more for ministers who felt they wanted to do better in terms of growing their church. I believe that we ought to prepare ministers to deal with the whole individual—body, mind, and spirit—so I supported that program and I was invited to California to participate in workshops and spiritual programs. I attended some of those sessions and met Greg. Greg was running those sessions. That was Greg's job, running that leadership program, getting their speakers lined up and setting up the programs. Greg later relocated to central Pennsylvania and set up the Cancer Recovery Foundation of America, an international organization. I've helped Greg to some extent over the years and greatly admire his work.

KW: How did Greg come to locate his foundation from California to central Pennsylvania?

GL: It was at my encouragement. Mary Jane and I helped Greg, his wife, and the foundation to come to Pennsylvania. I provided him with some financial and much moral support. I thought Greg had a very meaningful message that could help thousands of people struggling with all types of illness besides cancer. I also wanted Greg to work with people in Country Meadows Retirement Community. He did so then greatly expanded his work. Greg is now international though much of his work centers in North America. I am sure he has helped thousands recover and live healthy lives through physical, emotional, psychological, and spiritual healing. It is a message that I strongly believe in that transcends religion, ethnicity, and income.

KW: Did you have this philosophy of positive thinking and forgiveness before you met Greg or did you adopt this after you got involved with Crystal Cathedral?

GL: I had this philosophy to some extent. I've always been a pretty positive person. When I ran for governor, remember, it was generally conceded that that I didn't have a chance to win against the Republican machine. But I had had an interesting experience in running in 1952 for state treasurer and I had made a lot of friends out there. I learned to know a lot about the commonwealth and the problems of the various segments of the commonwealth, the various geographical areas. So I thought I would like to get the nomination. I was able to get the endorsement of what they then called the Policy Committee of the Democratic Party. I got that endorsement, and as a result, even though we had total budget of $2,500 in the primary, I won that primary by 60,000 votes. I had a very positive attitude. Most people thought that I was a throwaway candidate. I think the positive attitude that I had came through in my public appearances and in the media, the television, and the newspapers and radio stations. I think it affected the voting public. And, it may be one of the reasons why I won.

KW: Where did your positive attitude come from? Were you born with it? Were there people around you that influenced your thinking?

GL: My father had a very positive attitude. Dad started out as a young man in poor health. The fact is his health was bad enough that he couldn't continue as a country schoolteacher because, back in those days, country schoolteachers had to walk to the school about 6:00 in the morning, fire up the stove, and then go home and eat breakfast or take breakfast along. Dad had to walk a mile and a half or two miles a couple times a day and he couldn't do that. He had what they call Rheumatic Fever and his heart was affected. He made up his mind in business that he was going to try to supervise ten people rather than do ten people's work because he was in frail health. Dad was a very positive person. I think his positive attitude saw him through his illnesses and he had a great influence on me.

KW: Governor, how has that positive attitude and views on wellness impacted your life? After all, you are in your tenth decade and in great physical and mental health.

GL: I've had a fairly stressful life. You know, three years in the service. I had four years as governor. I struggled for at least five, six, seven years to get started in a new career, a significant career in long-term care, after I left the governorship. There were times that my wife and I were working 60 and 70 hours a week running a poultry farm and a hatchery. It was a bit of a struggle but I always had confidence that if we did a great job we'd make it. I know one person in health care once told me, "George, you don't care much about making money." I said, "Well, my attitude is this. If you do a great job in taking care of people in frail health, the money will take care of itself." And for us, it has. As long as one doesn't get greedy, like those fellows up on Wall Street, if you're willing to have a reasonable income rather than to rape the public and take a lot of money for services that you're not rendering, then you will do okay.

KW: Another person you were influenced by was Norman Vincent Peale and the Marble Collegiate Church in Manhattan.

GL: Yes. I've always learned from him and the philosophy of positive thinking. We had Norman Vincent Peale here to honor him in Hershey some years ago. I invited him and Mrs. Peale and spent some time with them. At that time he was building a long-term care facility in Pauling, New York. He wanted to learn more about our work in long-term care. I showed him and Mrs. Peale around and they liked it. One time I said to him, "Where do you get all those great stories that you use in your speeches?" He was a fabulous raconteur. He said, "Everybody has a good story." The more I thought about that, everybody does have a good story. Most people are too shy to tell it or too modest. But everybody has got at least one good story. Peale is the one who influenced me on positive thinking and Schuller and Greg Anderson influenced me on wellness and forgiveness. I've read most of Schuller's books, all of Anderson's books, and some of the books by Norman Vincent Peale. Peale, of course, got into the depths of the psychological aspect of religion during the Depression of the 30s when the Wall Street people who had lost their fortunes were jumping out of windows and committing suicide. He was counseling people. He got so busy counseling people who were considering suicide that he hired a full-time psychiatrist to help him. He developed and grew in the psychological component of the Christian religion. I've often said the amazing thing is that the psychology that Jesus taught is still relevant today and it's still as authentic today as it was when he taught it. I don't know how Jesus can be such a great psychiatrist unless God endowed him with a special skill, a special attribute. Jesus certainly attracted those great crowds for several reasons. Jesus did spiritual healing and healing of the body.

KW: Governor, do you think it's good for people to be around a lot of negativity?

GL: Well, I am reading a book on civility that points out that being around negative people is very bad for you. Yes, it can make it harder for you to stay on the positive side. If you can help them, that's fine; but negative people can have an unfortunate influence on you. People who can't sleep at night—if they're watching all kinds of bad shows, and I've watched Law & Order and that sort of thing—if you watch that kind of program and then go to bed, I think it's hard to get to sleep. I can have a hard time falling asleep after watching a program like that. And, there is way too much violence on TV these days. Our children are exposed to it at a very early age. Do you think that has any impact on the growing crime rate? I certainly do. Our brain is like a computer. You've got a trillion brain cells. Often I wonder how long it took the Creator to create a brain. I wonder if he could just snap his fingers and there were a trillion brain cells with all kinds of chemical actions in there, interrelating those brain cells to each other. Our brain cells try to sort out the positive from the negative. It is human nature to do so. Maybe some folks have brains that emphasize the positive while others emphasize the negative? I was listening to a man who does a program, he's on the faculty of Johns Hopkins, and he is an expert on civility. He said, "When you pat a dog's head, the dog's brain develops favorable chemicals"; it might be serotonin but I can't quite remember. And his studies showed that the person doing the patting has positive brain chemicals being released as well. Both the dog and the person benefit.

KW: Governor, in addition to wellness and positive thinking, what role has faith played in your life? You're a very spiritual person.

GL: Well, I'm still searching. I never reached a point where I figured that I had arrived. The Bible says "Now we see through a glass, darkly; but then face to face." But in religious matters I believe in being born again. However, being born again to me doesn't mean "Well I'm in great shape; I'm ready to appear before our Lord Jesus Christ." It means more because I am always working on being better at spirituality and helping my fellow man. When the Lord says to me, "George, what did you do with your life?" I'm ready to answer, "I think being saved means learning how to serve your fellow man—how to serve God through serving your fellow man. I've tried hard to do that but haven't been perfect." I wrote a little line once that went like this, "The sign of the saved is the love of the least and those are the ones who will be first at His feast." The sign of the saved is the love of the least. I'm reading a book right now where the author particularly emphasizes the fact that we need to serve others. We're put here on Earth to do God's work by serving our fellow man, by feeding the hungry, clothing the naked, giving drink to the thirsty, visiting the sick and imprisoned. That's what Jesus taught. If you're going to be saved, you need to work hard on all of those things. That's what Jesus would have done.

I think it's very hard to be a positive person unless you have a solid foundation of faith. I have had the bumps in the road. We all do. That's part of life and it's not easy. It is not pleasant. I guess God could have created us that everything is always pleasant, easy for us. But he didn't. There's a lot of stress in the world and I think a lot of sickness is a result of stress. Either stress from pollution in the air, or smoking, or eating the wrong kind of food or trying to work 20 hours a day. But if you don't have faith I think the stress is tremendously increased in your life. When you increase the stress, you're inviting problems, physical, mental, and spiritual. Faith is a spiritual medicine. It's a good thing. It takes a lot of faith sometimes to carry us through.

Also, you asked about what has influenced me. I have to mention that, in addition to Jesus Christ and the Bible, I went to Sunday school when I was a little boy. I had a Sunday school teacher whose name was Mrs. Franklin Menges. Her husband was the Congressman from our district. He was Republican and we were Democrats, but I think my mother and father voted for

Franklin Menges to go to the Congress. He was a fine man. A fine Christian gentleman. Mrs. Menges was just a darling woman. She was my Sunday school teacher and I think a lot of my faith began with her teaching.

KW: Did you ever have a conversion or a mystical experience?

GL: I don't know that I've every truly experienced what you are referring to. However, life's challenges have come close. Very close. We all go through those challenging times, particularly about the time we're in college and we wonder "What does this mean? How am I to live? What should I do with my life?" I've looked for answers and clear direction in those times. Somehow, God and Jesus have guided me. It has always worked—out mainly in service to others.

KW: When I hear you talk about these issues I hear a philosophy of wellness and positive thinking that you have practiced in your life and it dictates how you treat other people. Is that correct?

GL: I try to live that way. I try to. But of course, no one is perfect. I'm a very action-oriented person. I'm not a scholar. I do enjoy obtaining knowledge and I'd like to think I've accumulated quite a bit in 91 years! Knowledge to me is step one. If you don't have knowledge you don't have much capacity to serve mankind. The second step for me is to turn that knowledge into action. The way I've tried to turn it into action is to live out my Christian beliefs that God put me on this Earth to make a difference in the lives of others. History and historians, like you, will have to be the judge of my success.

KW: As you look back on your life, what are you most happy with?

GL: The Pennsylvania Dutch don't have a great capacity for happiness. They are a conservative lot. The Leaders were somewhat different. They *challenged complacency*. Of course I was born Pennsylvania Dutch. But I, somehow, secured the ability to want to be happy and enjoy life. I'd like to think that Mary Jane and my children and grandchildren are like that as well. I get great satisfaction from reaching goals—setting goals and reaching them. That's what makes me happy. That's where I get my great satisfaction and deep-down joy in life. I am also happy with being an entrepreneur, but not in the traditional sense. When we hear that term I think success is defined by making money. I'd like to think of myself as an entrepreneur in government, business, and helping the disenfranchised, the poor, those that society has dismissed. That, to me, is entrepreneurship. Not just making money. Sure, I've made money along the way but that has not been my primary goal in life.

KW: Do you ever see yourself just slowing down and just not doing anything?

GL: Well, I think the good Lord will let me know when that time comes. I'm sure there will come a time that I can't do what I'm doing now. I have a pretty good energy level. I'm pretty good until about 4 o'clock in the afternoon. Then, I start getting tired. And I'm sure the time will come that I'll get tired sooner than that. Maybe, one day, I'll read some of the books that I wanted to read for a long time and didn't get to it because I had too many irons in the fire.

KW: How is your physical health?

GL: I'm in pretty good shape. I have about five doctors. I've got a cardiologist, proctologist, dermatologist, neurologist, and a general practitioner. When I die the Hershey Medical Center may go bankrupt because they're going to lose one of their best customers! I have to stay around to keep that place prosperous! I plan to do just that. I do eat right. I very seldom eat a huge meal. I also exercise by walking a few times a week. I keep my mind stimulated.

KW: You told me once the essence of life is nonjudgmental, unconditional love.

GL: Yes, that's one of my favorites. I've learned about unconditional, nonjudgmental love over the years. I've experienced it and tried to live it out. That statement is engraved on my tombstone. It is quite egotistical, isn't it?!

KW: Do you think you've practiced that in your life?

GL: I've tried to, yes. I think the fact that I've been blessed with a long life, that I've had longevity, is from at least trying to live that out. I think the most devastating thing that you can do to yourself is anger and distrust. My wife says, "George, you trust everybody." She says, "You are too trusting." And I always say to her, "Mary Jane, yes I've trusted some people who were not trustworthy. Probably less than two percent of the people I've dealt with." But I said, "How much would I have lost in achieving things if I had not trusted the other 98 percent?" Everything in life depends on trust—marriage, children, business, the church. I once knew someone who said that they had two or three ministers who cheated on their wives while they were serving in his church. He had been active in the church; he sang in the church choir, he had been in the church counsel. He stopped going to church. I don't think he's gone to church since. Maybe he does now. But, he didn't go to church for a long time because he had ministers that were not trustworthy. Well, that was not a very wise decision, I think. And I think he would have been happier if he had not made that decision, if he tried to be nonjudgmental and realize that some people, even ministers, can be untrustworthy but they, too, need unconditional love. Maybe if they experienced unconditional love they wouldn't be so untrustworthy. I don't know but I think that might be true. I do believe unconditional, nonjudgmental love has a tremendous effect on our physical health, as well as our mental and spiritual health.

Under the glass top of my desk in the Governor's Office, I had a quote from Micah. "What does the Lord require of thee but to do justly, to love mercy, and to walk humbly with thy God?" I hope that sums up where I come from. I haven't always been perfect, I haven't always been right. I've made my share of mistakes.

Family

The Leaders are a close family. Mary Jane and George are the parents of four children: George Michael III, born April 19, 1945; Fred, born August 11, 1949, and passed away February 1, 2003; Jane, born February 12, 1954, while George was campaigning for the governorship; and David, born September 7, 1958, while the Leaders lived in the governor's residence. Besides supporting and encouraging one another in personal affairs, perhaps the true test of a family's successful interpersonal relations is the ability to get along in business affairs. Indeed, here the Leaders have been successful; in fact, collegial. Michael Leader is the president and CEO of Country Meadows Retirement Communities; David Leader serves as chief operating officer. Jane Leader Janeczek is responsible for special initiatives, and her husband, Ted, is executive vice president and chief financial officer.

Of course, George and Mary Jane have fostered this kind of relationship, being nurturing and encouraging parents. Governor Leader expressed the type of relationship they share when he described their calling practices: "I grew up in generation where it was common for family to drop in on one another without calling beforehand or prearranging a visit. This was often true even for neighbors when I was younger. You'd just stop by on a Sunday afternoon to chat, maybe share a cake or coffee. Well, today that is not very common at all. With how busy life has become it seems that even simple, short visits have to be prearranged. Cell phone, text messaging, meetings, appointments, all of seemingly necessary modes of communication may well have complicated life. To visit someone today, you must call ahead, get an appointment. In most cases our kids just drop by. Rarely do they have to call ahead. We live by that old tradition and I happy that we do."[3]

George and Mary Jane also have 12 grandchildren and one great-grandchild. Michael and Karen Leader's children are Jennifer, George Michael IV, Katelin, and Kristin. Jane and Ted Janeczek's children are Alex, Andrew, and Meredith. David and his wife Liesa Hall Leader have five adopted children. They are Tania, Ricardo, Grace, Catia, and Manuel (Xico). Finally, George and Mary Jane have one great-grandchild born in mid-2009, Kyle Lee Leader-Hamner.

Here, Governor Leader discusses family more thoroughly:

> KW: I want to discuss another subject that has great meaning to you. Family. Your children in particular. Let's start with your daughter.
>
> GL:[4] She was a very sweet little girl and she has grown into a wonderful human being. She had a blind brother by the name of Fred. Fred was a little older than she was. And, there was many a time that Fred took her hand or put his hand on her shoulder and she would lead him where we were going. That is among my best memories of Janie, especially as a child. She was four years younger than Fred and she was just a little girl and he was a pretty big fellow and she would help him. I think that's the happiest thought I have of her—how she would help her brother. She is very bright and did well in high school and graduated with good grades from Lafayette College. She and Ted have

three beautiful children. Janie is very active in the community. She works for political candidates during election season. She was vocal and a community leader years ago when there was the threat of Hershey Foods being sold off. That was, of course, defeated. She plays a role in Country Meadows working on special projects and her husband, Ted, is their financial officer and controller. Right now she is working on securing dogs for Country Meadows. Dogs are great pets and can do wonders for the guests as companions.

Let me give you an example of how Janie gets involved in things she believes in. Soon after President Obama finished his speech on Tuesday night (Obama's first presidential address to Congress in late February 2009) I quickly concluded that it was one of the best political speeches I ever heard and I've heard my share in 91 years. Well, Janie and I think alike. She called me after the speech and said, "Wasn't that a fantastic speech?" she said. "Wasn't he great?" And I said, "Yeah, I think it's one of the greatest speeches I've ever heard." Well, it is because of her belief in people like Obama and the possibility of change that is worth working for, she knocked herself out to work in that election for Obama (2008). Now, I was not that involved in it. I gave some money and I had originally supported Hillary Clinton. She was 20 or 30 points ahead in the polls when I gave her some money. Then this fellow came along and I listened to his speech on the steps of the old capitol in Springfield, Illinois, where he spoke for 45 or 50 minutes without notes or a teleprompter and delivered a message that would have done anyone proud. I said to Mary Jane, "You know, this man has a future. He has a gift. He's one of the best speakers I've heard in a long, long, long time." Well, I said, Janie participated in a group here in Derry Township and Dauphin County. They worked hard. They set up a telephone bank. They were on telephones three or four days before the election. I think something like 100 or 150 participated in those telephone banks—all volunteers. They all used their cell phones—and they all worked together—and they did a great job. Now, Janie is a—she's a liberal, I guess. I think you'd consider her a liberal. She is compassionate. When she believes in a cause she commits herself to it with no hesitancy, no reservations. That might sound like me! I guess I am biased. But she and her husband and family are good people. Decent people, concerned about the welfare of others. Sometimes, I think she takes after me because she can be a bit stubborn. Mary Jane tells me I am like that too particularly if I have an idea I want to pursue. I guess she is right! Anyway, Janie can be stubborn sometimes. I guess it is the Pennsylvania Dutch in her. We can all be stubborn sometimes!

KW: What's your happiest memory and thoughts about Fred?

GL: Maybe the greatest thing that happened to our family was having Fred. Fred taught us so much and stretched who we were as family in a good way. Fred was blind, of course. I guess it's true that people who lose one faculty, or fail to have one faculty, tend to have reinforcement in the others. Fred had a brilliant mind. He had almost total recall. He could remember things that I don't think the ordinary person could remember. He was a computer expert, a computer programmer. He could read the book of instructions (using Braille) on a computer program and practically recall not only the whole book, but the page and paragraph where the information was in the book. He had a genius for this. He was a straight A student all the time. He accomplished this through almost perfect recall. My wife read to him every night until eleventh grade. He'd go to bed about 10 o'clock, and if they hadn't finished what they were reading, they would get up at 6 o'clock and they'd finish it. I think I can say he never went to school unprepared. I guess if you never go to school unprepared it's not too hard to get As. Of course he had the retention to go with it. I think one of the nicest stories about Fred was that he was graduating from Swarthmore College with distinction in both math and science when federal government jobs were hard to come by. He wanted to work for the federal government. While Fred was trying to pursue a job in Washington our son, Michael, was working with a committee that was preparing the transition of the Washington, D.C., government from the hands of Congress to the people of Washington, D.C. Mike was working there and there were several other people working with him one of whom was a retired personnel man, I think from the Department of Agriculture. He knew all of the top personnel guys in the different departments. Michael had told him about his brother, Fred. Fred had taken the preadmission test for the federal government and got a 97.5 out of 100. Well, the man from Agriculture told Michael, "I think I could help him. Let me write a couple letters." So, he wrote a couple of letters to these department heads about Fred, put some things in about him personally. Meanwhile, Fred got a job as a GS5 in the Department of the Navy as a civilian. About two months later the Department of Agriculture sent him a letter that said "We're accepting you for a job as a GS7." Now remember, he had GS5 in the Navy and then Agriculture offered him GS7 probably because of the influence of the man that Michael knew. I told Fred, "Well, just write a nice letter of gratitude to the Navy and tell them that you've had a better offer over at Agriculture, and you're going to go over there." Fred said, "Oh, no. I gave the people in the Navy my word that I'm going to take that job." He said, "I'm not going to take the Agriculture job. I don't want favoritism or people to think that I got a job because I know someone." Now that showed a type of character. The difference in salary between a GS5 and a GS7 was considerable and it would be a considerable amount of time before he would become a GS7 in the Navy. As it turned out, he did well in the Navy and it wasn't too long until he had two excellent service awards in the Navy. They didn't just give you a certificate, but they had added a bonus to his salary for the rest of your career.

KW: Fred had a fairly lengthy career with the federal government, didn't he?

GL: He had 25 years with the Navy and later transferred from down there in Georgetown to up here to Mechanicsburg. I guess they knew he was blind up here and, initially, they figured that a blind person wouldn't be of much help to them in Mechanicsburg. So, he had a hard time getting the transfer. Well, sometimes I'm not shy about trying to throw my weight around. So, while he was trying to get a transfer I said, "Fred, I know the Congressman, Bill Goodling, and his father. The Goodling family knew the Leader family for two or three generations at least. Why don't I get a hold of the Congressman and see if he can't get things loosened up." Fred responded immediately, "No, no, no. Don't you do that. I don't want you to do anything like that at all. Don't use your influence. I'll get there eventually, just leave it alone." So, it took about two years and he was transferred to Mechanicsburg. He got to be one of their key people. He was the kind of person that if they got stuck on a Saturday or a Sunday, and they'd send for him, and his wife would drive him up to Mechanicsburg, he'd stay until they solved the problem, then he'd go home. He had a fantastic capacity. I don't know what being blind had to do with it—probably something—but he was remarkable. I think he had one test that showed his IQ up around 160, which is pretty good.

Well, Fred passed away in 2003 from a heart condition. We miss him terribly but know that he is with the Lord.

KW: Let's turn to David. What are some of your fondest memories with David?

GL: David had five parents. He had his mother and his father and he had a sister and two brothers that helped to raise him. He was born while I was governor. It was very rare for a governor to have a newborn. He was probably the most lovable child that I've ever known. That's what I recall about him most, especially as a child. I know that when I was on the road—I hate to say it, I wouldn't want Mary Jane to hear this because she might think I drove dangerously—but I would try to get home if it was a long day, I would try to get home before David went to bed so I could be with him at least a little. He was a remarkable child. We would read together, play outside together. Holidays were special with all of the children but I particularly remember how excited David would get at Christmas. He gave and received love in a remarkable measure from the whole family. He still, he is still a sweet, compassionate person—very generous. He does things that I can't believe. I think he must have robbed a bank, because I don't know where he gets money to do some of the things he does. Unfortunately his first marriage didn't work out. His first wife was from Portugal and she has returned there. They adopted children from the Azores. He and his former wife remain friendly. He has remarried. I think he's very happy. They are a great example. His wife, as a single mother, went to China to adopt a little girl. Now David has officially become that little girl's father. David works as an executive for Country Meadows. Several years ago he joined the company. We are glad that he is with us here. He's a very bright person and helps Michael, who is the CEO of Country Meadow, with many issues and programs. He checks in on his mother regularly. We look forward to his visit.

KW: Let's turn to Michael. You have described him to be as your alter-ego.

GL: Well, Michael started as a combination of Mary Jane and me. He is a little more conservative, like his mother. He doesn't make the quick decisions I make. But he makes good decisions. He took over Country Meadows ten years ago. I promised that I would step down as CEO when I turned 80 in 1998. I did. Michael had been the president of Country Meadows. He then became CEO. We had a good organization when I left and it's a better organization now thanks, in large measure, to Michael. He has 65 people at the corporate level and he's probably got all the specialties in long-term care covered. If I need an expert to work with me on an issue at Providence Place, I can count on Michael to lend me an expert. That's one of the places I go because he's got specialists. We've got some of the best brains in long-term care, I think, in the nation. And they're doing a great job.

KW: What's one or two of your fondest memories with Michael—growing up, when he was younger?

GL: He was the only child we had for four years. He was very close to Mary Jane and me because he was the only child for four years. We gave him a lot of time and attention. I remember we were living out on the Willow Brook Farm and we had about two acres of lawn and a big heavy steel-wheeled lawnmower. I gave him $2 to cut the grass. He was about 8 or 10 years old. He could hardly turn the mower around. The perspiration would be running down his poor little face and my in-laws thought I was terrible to let him do that. I don't think Mary Jane was too pleased either. But he loved it: working and earning a few dollars. He spent a lot of time with us in the poultry business at Willow Brook. We'd be traying up eggs for the incubator and he'd be down on the floor with a tray, putting eggs on a tray when he was just a little fellow. The eggs were just about the size that he could hold them in his little hands. He'd drop one once in awhile and we'd watch him out of the corner of our eye, but we'd just let him go on. I used to kid him. I used to say, "Michael"— when he was directing his brothers and sisters, I'd say, "Michael, remember, you're not the father of this family, you're only the assistant father." So I had to chastise him a little bit, because sometimes he thought that he was the father! He grew up and matured very rapidly. He was a very responsible little guy, he really was, and part of the team. I remember by the time he was in high school, that would have been in the early 1960s, he began to help me in long-term care. I remember one Saturday we went out and raked some lawn, seeded some lawn at Leader Nursing and Rehabilitation Center in Camp Hill. He helped me do those kinds of things that are very memorable, working together as father and son. When he was in college he would substitute for administrators when they would go out on vacation in the summer. He could take responsibility at a very early age. I said there was a time in his life when he felt if he didn't get to be governor by the time he was 40, he was a failure. But he got over that and I think he's happy with what he's doing now.

KW: Do you think that the philosophy of life that you and Mary Jane share has been an influence on your children?

GL: If they don't get it from your example as their parents they're not going to get it, because a lot of times children don't hear what you're saying, but they can see what you're doing. I'm really pleased that my children are all very personally charitable. Our companies are charitable, too, but a lot of people substitute company charity for personal charity. We have company charity. Country Meadows gives 10 percent of its pretax income to charity. Every one of my children and Mary Jane have their own charities in addition to that. And I'm proud of that. They're very compassionate people. I said, if you want to go in the trucking business, you don't have to have a lot of compassion but, hopefully you have decent ethical standards. However, if you want to be in long-term care you've got to have some motivation beyond just making money. Tragically, too many people got into long-term care only to make money. I don't think that the Leaders did that. Money wasn't our primary motivation.

The Governor's view on wellness, spirituality, and family extend to his views on political and social issues as well, as discussed in the following chapter.

Notes

1. George M. Leader, interview with Kenneth C. Wolensky, March 26, 2009, Hershey, PA.
2. Greg, a survivor of lung cancer, is the founder of the Cancer Recovery Foundation of America and an author on cancer and recovery. See http://www.cancerrecovery.org
3. Untaped conversation with author, October 6, 2009.
4. George M. Leader, interview with Kenneth C. Wolensky, February 25, 2009, Hershey, PA.

6

Views, Philosophies, and Ideas about Contemporary Issues

Throughout his life Governor Leader has willingly expressed his views about political, social, economic, and human rights issues. Certainly this was true during his tenure in elected office. Seldom has he been less than outspoken in his private life. His values are mainly derived from his life experiences and have been extended into his stance on civic issues. It runs contrary to Pennsylvania German culture that one expresses his or her views on public issues, seldom even privately. When it comes to self-expression, however, George Leader hasn't always been a compliant Pennsylvania Dutchman.

For example, he has remained a stalwart liberal and progressive both historically and contemporarily. Such a political philosophy isn't consistent with most of Pennsylvania's history. Indeed, such views are contradictory to much of the dominant thinking in American political and social culture in the closing decades of the twentieth century and in the early twenty-first century. He hasn't been swayed, however. He has often expressed views that the so-called mainstream of American political culture calls out of step and what the right wing of American political culture would likely attack. Indeed, it seems that in American politics the terms liberal and progressive have somehow become dirty words. Leader's values, however, have outweighed any desires to be conformist with the dominant narrative of society. Finally, in what some might consider the era of strict individualism, greed, and winner-take-all economics of the current period George Leader has consistently remained generous, supportive of those in need, and empathetic of those that can't always conform to the demands of American society. When questioned about his views he often explains that he is trying hard to live out his Christian beliefs though his actions, he says, are imperfect. And, when pressed about from where these views are derived, he points to the Bible, his father and family, the traditions of American progressive agrarian politics, President Franklin Delano Roosevelt, Governor Gifford Pinchot, and the experiences of ordinary people whom he has encountered through his life.

Governor Leader's brother Henry (who served as legislative secretary from 1955 to 1959) explains the derivation of the family political philosophy:

KW: Why were the Leaders Democrats?

HL:[1] By the time I was conscious of politics, it was an intellectual commitment. It was a policy commitment. I assume that the very beginning of it may have been an inheritance from my father and his father who were always Democrats. My grandfather had served on the York Township school board. My father was active in education and other social issues. Their involvement influenced the whole family. We were Democrats from the time we knew anything at all about politics. Of course, we were very, very committed to Franklin Roosevelt, who is the first of the presidents that meant anything to me. I was born in 1922. By the time Roosevelt took office in 1933 I was ten years old and I was very aware—we were all very aware of that election. By the time Roosevelt came along we were all ardent Roosevelt people.

KW: Why Roosevelt?

HL: What he was doing was consistent with our philosophy. Dad was a great believer in the common man and he was very much interested in their struggles. We were born and raised liberals. It was philosophical. We were strongly in favor of the kinds of things that Roosevelt stood for. It was a populist appeal. Farm Democrats. I don't remember any political groups or organizations other than the Democratic Party that were involved in "common man" issues when I was a youth. We weren't in the labor movement or some farm political movement or anything of that sort but my father understood such views and was empathetic to them. My father was a pretty good guy in terms of morality and thought that the system should work for people at large not the special interests or the well healed. By the time I was in high school—it would have been the 1936 election when Roosevelt secured a second term—I was betting other kids that he would win. I was betting with dozens of Republican kids. Kids at the high school age, for instance, were deeply involved in the election. One guy even slapped me in the face because he didn't agree with my views! I ended up dating his sister for a couple of years. Her mother broke that up, probably *because* of my politics. But we were highly involved. I made nickel and dime bets. I had one fifty-cent bet. I made seven or eight dollars on betting on Roosevelt in 1936. Pretty good money for a teenager in the Depression!

KW: Do you think that the morality and class issues helped to define your brother's politics, especially the time that he served as governor?

HL: Oh, I think so. I think it was *always* central to our view of democratic politics. We were aware of class and race. George felt a moral obligation to make things work in the interest of all the people. There was always a moral component.

The Leader children, Michael, Jane, and David, explain that their father's views and passions are derived from family experience, breadth of knowledge, and intellectual curiosity. They, too, explain his risk-taking and how that may relate to his outspokenness on issues that he often exhibited in public forums.

KW: What, do you think, influenced your father's thinking?

Michael Leader:[2] Definitely his father, Guy. And his political views were influenced by his father as well. He was a very moral man and that influenced Dad as well.

Dad has been a risk-taker and that's certainly influenced his views. He certainly has never been afraid to express his views. I don't think he saw himself as a risk taker but many of the things that he's done over the years have been pretty risky. That goes back to a young age. He once told me that when he was a boy, when he was attending York High School and York Collegiate Institute, that his father had given him a car to commute to town. When he was playing football YCI played against the Gettysburg freshmen and they used to race. He said we raced all the way from

York against some other guys who were driving to Gettysburg, all the way from York to Gettysburg in cars to see who could get there first. That was, obviously, a dangerous thing to do. He talked about going 80 miles per hour in those old cars! Now, if his father ever found out Dad would have been in quite a bit of trouble. He was willing to accept risks to have fun, to be engaged in politics, and to excel in business. I don't know whether psychologically there's some relationship there between someone willing to race from York to Gettysburg and political and business ventures. I suspect so. The other thing I remember doing was traveling with my Dad when I was quite young. Especially in the years immediately after the governorship when I was in my early teens, Dad did a considerable amount of public speaking and fundraising particularly for Jewish organizations. He was passionate about that. He still is. Sometimes my mother was not able to go with him and he would enlist me to go along. I couldn't drive. But I could go out with him and just sit in the audience. On the way to an engagement he wouldn't talk. He would be going over his speech; he would be preparing it mentally. I would hear him speak. He was very effective and passionate. On the way home, we'd have a chance to talk and he would often reiterate his views with me.

Jane Leader Janeczek: Dad reads a very broad range of material. He keeps informed and that influences him tremendously. There are very few subjects he doesn't know something about. It's amazing to me. He also follows sports; he loves sports competition and is a big Phillies fan. Dad has unconditional love for the masses, for the disenfranchised, for the special needs kids, for the African American disenfranchised, for the gay population, for the oppressed anywhere.

David Leader: He gets *Discovery Magazine*, the *New York Times*, and other publications. Every week Michael, David, and I receive articles, magazines, and newspapers that he sends to us that he thinks we should read. Always a new idea.

Governor Leader explains his political philosophy and his views on several issues:

KW: I want to ask you about your political beliefs. You've remained liberal and fairly progressive over a lot of years when, especially the Democratic Party, and American society as a whole has gotten conservative. How do you explain your beliefs?

GL:[3] Well, I'm pragmatic. In politics you are always dealing with the need to have a majority. That's the way it works. Someone said democracy is the worst form of government except for all the others. I recognize the need to have a majority. I think, for example President Clinton took us pretty well toward the middle and that's why he was successful. I always say he stole a good chunk of the Republican program. That's one of the reasons he was successful. Certainly things like the trade program—NAFTA—that was essentially a Republican program. That certainly couldn't be considered a Liberal-Democratic program and yet he supported that. Whether in the long run that's going to be a blessing or a curse to America, I don't know. Right now, it's some of each. But I think as a governor I was a liberal but I was also moderate on some issues. I'm proud of the fact that when my administration had to borrow money through our authorities we had as low a rate of interest as any other industrial state in the nation, lower than some. So fiscally, I was a moderate. Socially, my programs that helped industry would have been considered Socialist by some of my conservative Republican friends. But we did some liberal things. Let's face it: no chief executive in America—including the president—has total power. I always say I'd like to be a dictator but nobody ever elected me a dictator. When you're in a democracy, there are limits. I say we probably got 80 percent of our progressive programs through the legislature in spite of the fact that we, the Democrats, never controlled the Senate and we only controlled the House of Representatives for two years. Progressivism and liberalism are almost unheard of in Pennsylvania, then and now. So, I guess, we were unusual.

KW: Pennsylvania's twentieth-century governors have been referred to as "thinkers" or "doers"—seldom both. You and Gifford Pinchot seem to have been both. You thought things through, and accomplished a good deal. How do you feel about that characterization?

GL: I like to believe it's accurate. It was one of the most satisfying things that was ever said about my performance in government. I have a very active mind. My mind is active from the time I get up in the morning until the time I go to bed at night. Not all of my ideas are blockbusters and I'm more than willing to sit down with people who are more knowledgeable in a field than I am. I kick the idea around without limits. I said, "When I get a great idea before breakfast in the morning, and then I go to my office and I start talking with people who have knowledge in that field, I never wind up with the same idea; I always wind up with a *better* idea." There's something constructive about two or three or four people kicking an idea around and having to defend your position and keeping your mind open for discussion. Stimulation between minds always generates something better or almost always generates something better than one mind alone. Your ideas need to be put to the test in a good challenging situation. I was lucky in government to have some people around me who were very bright, very able, and didn't hesitate to differ with me. If you just surround yourself with "yes" people, they're never going to bring out the best in you and you're never going to do the best job you're capable of doing. You need that challenge. I had a lot of wonderful people in Harrisburg and we drew on a lot of top-notch consultants and we learned from them. We were able to, thanks to the School of Local and State Government at Penn, we were able to tap into some of the best brains in America in sixty plus fields of endeavor. And if I belong as both a thinker and a doer it's because first of all, I had a good "kitchen cabinet"; secondly I had a good general cabinet, and third, we tapped the best brains in America and we didn't sit on their ideas. With me there's a very short period of time between getting an idea shaped up and then carrying it out. I'm not the type that enjoys just talking about an idea. I like to carry them out.

Public Education

KW: I know one of your areas of interest and activity is education. Explain your views on this topic.

GL: Absolutely. You can't teach people what they don't want to learn. We are trying to teach people—especially in the secondary and postsecondary system—what most of them don't want to learn. That's why, when they hit puberty especially, they lose interest. Many young people, especially in the inner cities, lose interest in learning. When I was at the University of Pennsylvania we talked about individual differences and yet we have an education system that doesn't respect those differences. Every student has to meet the same standards. What does the system do to tap in to their individual skills and talents? Not very much

Views, Philosophies, and Ideas about Contemporary Issues / 143

in my view. I'm probably the only person you've ever met who's against pushing our students to do more math and science. We only need 15 or 20 percent math and science students. You can be a success in life without being a master of math and science. I think many students get bored with math and science. Maybe that's why they lose interest in learning. The education system does a poor job of capturing their interests at critical moments in their lives. My father always taught me that America is a great melting pot. America is a great melting pot because of the public school system. In most areas, that's true. In the inner cities we integrated schools about 50 years ago. African Americans were put into the white schools and white people moved to the suburbs. They called it "white flight." Right here in Harrisburg, our state capital, in 15 or 20 years, about 90 percent of the white people moved to the West Shore, on the west side of the Susquehanna River. So we integrated the black and white folks but the system disintegrated. That left us with low-income people in the city. I had a program in the Harrisburg schools for four or five years, and 70 to 75 percent of the students were dropping out around the ninth and tenth grade. I have a prison education program. They say our prisons are 50 percent white and 50 percent African American and other races and ethnicities, such as Hispanics. I can tell you that in my classes where I'm training mentors to teach Christianity in the prisons they are more like 75 or 80 percent non-white. I don't know where all the white people in prison are hiding. The prison program I run is called Second Chance Ministries. More on that later. I think that we have the majority of minorities in the decaying inner cities or in prison. I don't know.

KW: Do you think that public education has changed in 50 years?

GL: Well, if I may disagree with you, it hasn't changed enough. No one can tell me that you can't teach students in the inner city *something*. It's the fact that what we're presenting to them is not of interest to them. Then they fail; they do failing work for one or two years, and then they drop out because they say "I'm never going to graduate anyhow." So they drop out. Now they're on the street. They have no marketable skill. They're sitting ducks for the drug people. I've heard it said that drug people say that "If they arrest one of our boys on the street, we'll have him replaced within two weeks." Or they steal automobiles or something else. They wind up in jail and if they're sentenced to more than two years, they wind up in the state system—which we call the State

Correctional Institution—SCI. Well, they don't correct much of anything, in many cases, because they're so limited in the amount of personnel they have to train these people to adjust to a productive life. They come out on the street with $50 or $75 in their pocket, and aren't allowed to drive an automobile for six months and they can't get a job because they're considered dangerous. The chance of their being rehabilitated is certainly not good. Not good at all. The tragedy is that when these young men get sentenced to prison for five or ten years when they do come out 60 percent of them are going to be back in prison again within three years. So, when you start a life in prison as a young man there's a pretty good chance you'll be going back to prison on a regular basis for the rest of your life. The more you're institutionalized the greater the likelihood that you'll never be able to adjust to the outside world where you'll have to make a lot of decisions for yourself. Chances are you're going to make poor decisions because you haven't learned a better way. Maybe if we offered them the opportunity to learn life skills in the schools and early in life they wouldn't end up in prison. I think our public education system, while it has done a lot of good, focuses too much on standardizing every student, not developing their talents, and overlooks the needs of minorities. Not every child is the same. They don't learn the same ways. So, why does the educational system treat them all the same?

Corrections and the Prison System

KW: You are very concerned about those in the correctional system. Explain that?

GL: When I started Second Chance Ministries in 1997 was had 37,500 in prison (State Correctional Institutions, not including county jails or federal penitentiaries in Pennsylvania). Now we're up to 47,500 and, by the way, that's as many patients as we had in mental hospitals in the 1950s and now that number has dropped to less than 8,000. The projection is that, in the next six or eight years, Pennsylvania correctional facilities will have to build 10,000 more cells and the state—not including the counties or cities—will have a prison population exceeding 60,000. We should be ashamed about that! But have you ever heard a politician say "we have too many people in prison?" The state system alone costs taxpayers over $2 billion a year now and $26,000 per inmate per year. That's about the cost of a Penn State four-year education. If we were turning people's lives around the corrections money would be money well spent. Unfortunately, we're not turning their lives around. The new cells are going to cost maybe forty-five or fifty thousand dollars a year to operate until they're amortized. New York State has just taken a drastic step—and some of the other states—to try to do more of what they call intermediate punishment where inmates are granted probation and have to get a job. They're required to get a job, and they're required to pay part of the cost of their probation officer. Isn't that a better system that locking them up for a long time?

I must say that I blame some of my good Christian friends for this who say "Lock 'em up and throw the key away." If society had a better position on the treatment of those who've done wrong and deserve a second change then the politicians, who aren't stupid, would listen. We have judges who say they are tough on crime. Well sure they're tough on crime. They're not paying for it. We are and the judges are getting handsome salaries to populate the prisons!

KW: Previously I asked you about the death penalty and executions while you were governor. Can you expand on your views?

GL: As I've gotten more wisdom I've come to conclude that no person has the right to decide that another person should die as a result of a conviction in a capital case. I don't agree with the death penalty. I don't think it is humane or Christian. It is certainly inconsistent with the Bible. There is now so much DNA evidence that has proven that some convicted killers are innocent. That is enough to say that the death penalty is inherently wrong.

KW: However, you signed death warrants and the commonwealth executed nine capital cases during your term as governor.

GL: You are correct. I did sign death warrants and there were executions. They were probably the most difficult decisions I ever had to make. I tried to do it with a clear conscience but that was almost impossible—I can tell you that it bothers me to this day. I am sorry for signing the warrants and that executions were carried out under my watch. I can only ask that God forgive me for doing so. When I stand before God I am going to make my repentance known. I am sincerely sorry.

Politics

KW: I'd like to turn to your memories of prominent politicians that you knew as well as your views on the current political environment. First, there aren't many governors around today who had relationships with politicians from the 1950s and 1960s. Let's start with an individual that you knew and admired. In fact, you toured with him in Pennsylvania. What was the appeal of Jack Kennedy?

GL: Well, I remember Jack Kennedy when he was running and I remember—Lyndon Johnson was running at that time, too. I supported Kennedy because there were a lot of things I liked about him. I certainly didn't like his father. Frankly, I thought he was a crook—bootlegging for example. Harry Truman expressed the attitude of all of us when someone asked him, "Are you concerned about the Pope if Kennedy is elected president?" He said, "No, I'm not concerned about the Pope, I'm concerned about the Pop." I was also concerned about Joe Kennedy because he had to have a great working relationship with the mob to bring all that whiskey in from Canada. Otherwise they would have killed him. Not only would they have killed him, they might have killed some members of his family. But he was certainly paying off the mob all he time he was bringing that whiskey in, and making all that easy money. Then, of course, he rode the stock market in the 1920s and made money. When Roosevelt made him the head of the Securities and Exchange Commission someone said "Why would he put a man like Kennedy in there?" He said, "Well, he certainly knows all the tricks of the trade. So he should be able clean it up." I don't know if he did or not, he must have done all right.

In any case, Jack Kennedy held many good ideas and I agreed with most of them. The value of public service, for example, and the good that can be done by government; advancement of civil rights, though he was somewhat slow in advancing a civil rights bill that Johnson later signed, and professionalizing the federal government. Isn't it remarkable how these views have changed in American society in the last few decades? Who, today, thinks government can do any good? Well, I certainly do.

Kennedy was good for the Democratic Party. In some ways he continued the tradition of Roosevelt and, in many ways he redefined the leadership of the party with his youthfulness and vigor. Of course, we know now that he had a very active private life that I won't get into.

KW: You've talked about your relationship with Adlai Stephenson, who ran for president twice in the 1950s. How was your relationship with him?

GL: I certainly supported Adlai. Adlai decided to launch his campaign in Harrisburg in 1956 at our state Democratic annual dinner and I introduced him and the Democratic Party bought a half-hour time on national television for him. He stayed with us in the governor's mansion. Adlai had worked on his speech that night and he worked all day the next day. He was still making changes on that speech right up to speech time. His delivery was fair. My introduction was short. He was quite lengthy. Too lengthy. He was such a perfectionist. An intellectual perfectionist that wasn't satisfied with anything. The draft he started with was probably written by Arthur Schlesinger or someone like that and he just kept rewriting and rewriting and correcting and adjusting. I think he shortened his life. It's hard to live as a perfectionist and it's hard to live *with* a perfectionist. It is too bad because he was a great man. He was a great thinker. He probably would have been a lousy president because I don't think a meticulous person like that can make all of the decisions on a timely basis. I think the president by necessity, much of the time, has to paint with a broad brush. You can't do all that nitty gritty stuff that he considered so important. He was also very sensitive. I remember I was having breakfast with him in New York at one of the big hotels. It might have been the Waldorf Astoria. And, he had just been quoted on something on some foreign policy matter, which was not earthshaking. But, during breakfast he was worried and grieving over the fact that they hadn't properly stated his position and he was going to put another statement out correcting his position. I said to him, "Governor, don't you know if you put a correction out, you're just going to call more attention to it?" In politics sometimes you've just got to swallow hard. But, he couldn't let it go. I learned from experience that, sometimes, you just have to let it go. Numerous times, when I held a press conference, I used to say, "I wonder how that is going to play back." I knew I'd done my best, but I couldn't determine how it was going to play back. And many times it's twisted or turned and badly quoted. I helped as much as I could with Adlai's campaigns. For example, we were having a governor's conference in Chicago and he invited my wife and me down to his farm, which was near Springfield. I couldn't get over that land out there, that farmland. So level and the topsoil was so black and fertile. He invited us down for lunch and he said, "I'd like to ask a favor of you." He said, "I'd like to have your Secretary of the Commonwealth, Jim Finnegan, to be my campaign manager. And I'd like to ask Matthew McCloskey to be my finance chairman." Matthew McCloskey was one of the two largest builders in Philadelphia. Finnegan was a fine Democratic party man and well known. "Well you couldn't get a finer man than Jim Finnegan," I said, "he's my Secretary of the Commonwealth and he's just as fine as the good Lord can make them." I said, "as far as McCloskey is concerned, he'll do a good job for you and he won't do anything to embarrass you." That's asking a lot of a finance chairman because there was lot of money out there that's a little on the shady side. He did select those two and so I supported him before that, and I certainly would have supported him after that, if I hadn't supported him before.

KW: What was your relationship with Lyndon Johnson?

GL: In my view Lyndon was a tyrant. Very controlling and he could be nasty if he didn't get his way. I agreed with many of his policies on social issues. But his personality was my polar opposite. When I was running for U.S. Senator in 1958 the Democrats had a television studio in Washington, D.C. where candidates made films that would be aired on television. I went down there to make some films with Senator Joe Clark. So, we invited Lyndon Johnson, who at that time was the majority leader, and asked whether he'd do a film endorsement. He came right off the floor of the Senate. He hardly knew me. He did a taping with an endorsement. He asked one of my staff people, "Why would Leader want me in an endorsement?" The staff person told him, "Well, because you've got a lot of influence in Pennsylvania." At that stage of his career he wasn't a terribly popular person. But, he was a major leader of the Senate and he was running for president, of course, in 1960. When Jack Kennedy chose Lyndon as his running mate he did so because Jack Kennedy thought he figured out where the electoral votes were going to come from—and he had to have Texas to win. I appreciated the endorsement but never could quite understand Lyndon Johnson. I'll tell you another story about Lyndon Johnson. When he was first elected to the Senate we had just elected a senator from Pennsylvania by the name of Frank Myers, a friend of mine, a wonderful man, a fine Christian gentleman. He went to Washington and they made him chairman of the committee to go down and investigate the election in Texas that sent Lyndon Johnson to the Senate. He came back and said, "Oh, yes there was some sheriff down there that stole a county for him." The Senate delayed seating Johnson but Myers helped him to be seated because the Democrats needed another Democrat in the Senate. Well, as a reward for that, by the end of his first term, Frank Myers was made Assistant Majority Leader in the Senate in his first term. Ordinarily it would have taken four or five terms to get there. Johnson had that sway and power. Of course, so did the senior Democratic senators who, I am sure, viewed it as a debt paid to Frank Myers. I do believe stress shortens people's lives—Frank later developed leukemia and he was getting blood transfusions. Frank died in his second term. I admired Frank but always questioned his motivations in working to seat Johnson who was probably elected dishonestly as U.S. Senator from Texas.

KW: Do you think politics can be corrupting?

GL: No doubt. Politics—big city politics—is a corrupting influence, I think. That doesn't say we're saints out here in the country. But we have small sins out here. They have big sins in the city, I think. I guess the opportunities are greater, I don't know. Right now State Senator Vincent Fumo (D-Philadelphia) is under indictment and will probably be convicted on some one hundred counts of corruption. I'm sure he has made quite a few mistakes, if you call them mistakes, over the years—and he will very likely wind up in prison for them. Some would say he was simply bringing home the bacon. Others say—including the federal prosecutor—that he padded himself and his friends in the process. Apparently that is the case but he is innocent until proven guilty (Fumo was convicted in the summer of 2009 on all counts and sentenced to five years in prison).

KW: I want to ask you about current affairs. There is much in the news now about the economy. We're in a troubled time right now with the U.S. economy. The job reports aren't good, the gross domestic product reports aren't good. You lived through one depression. Here we are in another serious recession. What do you make of what's happening right now and how do you compare that to the 1930s?

GL: Well, there are a lot of similarities in terms of the fact that it was due to greed on Wall Street and the abuse of credit. Some of those hedge funds had borrowed—for every dollar that they put up—they borrowed up to $45. Back in the 30s, anybody could borrow money. My attorney general was a young man when the Depression struck. By the age of 29, he was worth a million dollars. I said, "Two questions, Herb. Where did you get the money? And how could you be so smart?" He said, "Anybody could get the money." He said you could take a pencil and come down on the financial page and pick a stock that way, and buy it. Because he said they were all going up. But then, when the stock market went broke, he lost his home and everything. He and his wife and their baby had to move home to his mother because she still had a roof over her head. She was widowed, but she had a roof over her head. He had a million dollars at the age of 29 in 1929, and he lost everything, including his home. Now, some of those people up there on Wall Street who were billionaires if they had it in stock, some of that stock now is almost worthless, if not worthless. Greed. One thing I've learned in my 91 years is that greed is a very dangerous component in one's life. Sooner or later, if you have enough greed, it will bring its own punishment. You're going to get in trouble. Greed. I said those people on Wall Street were willing to destroy the economy of the world, just at the time when we were becoming prosperous enough to feed the hungry in Africa, send medicine to the sick in Africa, just at that time, in order to get a few more zeroes behind the line stating their net worth. They were willing to jeopardize the economy of the whole world. And they did. A lot of them brought on their own punishment, because some of them are broke now. Greed is a terrible sin. It's a sin against ourselves as much as a sin against mankind.

KW: Do you think we'll recover from it?

GL: Oh, I think we'll recover. I don't know if I'll live long enough to see it. But I think there's a chance that we'll be out of it in 2 or 3 years, and there's a chance that it will take 10 or 15 or 20 years. No one knows for sure. I think we'll make every effort to keep it as short as possible because – well we already have three or four million people out of work.

KW: Governor, I want to ask you these two questions. You probably are the single person alive today—certainly in Pennsylvania—who was been involved in politics and public affairs for over 60 years. Given your experience, how is the Democratic

Party of today, in 2009, different from when you were very actively involved in the Democratic Party?

GL: Well, when I started the state was Republican in registration by nearly a million registrants. By the early 1960s the state was Democratic by 600,000. When I was in politics the suburbs were still voting Republican. Now the suburbs are voting Democratic in many cases. That's a tremendous change and I can't tell you exactly why that change took place because the suburbs tend to be middle and upper-middle income people. Why those people are voting Democratic—even electing Democratic congressmen, as well as casting majority votes for state-wide Democratic candidates—I don't quite understand why except that, I hope, they are a little more open in their views. I don't know that their positions on social matters changed that much, except a lot of those people probably are not conservatives on the social issues, like abortion, same-sex marriage, and issues like that. With regard to abortion, for example, they're usually for free choice. They are for gun control, probably. They probably don't care about same-sex marriage, one way or the other. These are the things that Republicans are making a big deal of that seem to be more appealing to higher income people, conservative, religionists, and, pardon me, to less sophisticated people. I think more moderate voters found, on such issues, the Democratic Party was a lot more sophisticated. Their candidates were a lot more sophisticated on those subjects. Maybe that is part of it. But it's hard to believe that the blue states had become quite so blue. I think a lot of it was in the suburbs and, of course, the cities. I think we Democrats still lose a lot of the rural votes; we still do well in the inner cities, particularly with the minorities. I think Obama got 90 percent of the African American vote, for example. But it has changed. The nature and makeup of the Democratic Party is entirely different than what it was when I was a candidate. I had to get a lot of votes in what we called out here the "Bible Belt," and I did get them because I came from out of there and I understood those people. They trusted me.

KW: You are a very progressive person. You were a progressive governor in the tradition of a Gifford Pinchot. Do you think the Democratic Party has gotten more progressive, less progressive, about the same?

GL: Some of the elements are more progressive, but fiscally, I'm a moderate. I feel the extreme left has a tendency to spend more than we have and our grandchildren will have to pay for it. I'm amazed that the (George W.) Bush administration was able to run up the deficit so much in a Republican party dominated by conservative people. Does that make sense? So-called fiscal conservatives bankrupted the federal government! Why aren't people protesting that? I will never understand how the Bush administration screwed up so badly on the fiscal end of things. I said the Liberals tend to spend more than we have. Well, recently, it was the conservatives that spent too much that we didn't have. That amazes me. The conservatives have a tendency not to feed the poor if they can help it. I said the liberals think that everybody ought to have a good job. The conservatives feel everybody ought to have at least enough to buy sandwiches and live in a shack. The Independents think we ought to give them something but not too much. The poor people in the street should have at least a sandwich, a blanket, and a box to sleep in. They haven't committed themselves to anything. But the liberals tend to go overboard. Some of the extreme liberals go too far. We need moderate conservatives and moderate liberals because somebody is going to win and somebody's going to have to do the job. I'm a moderate Liberal. Democrats today are embarrassed to call themselves liberal. I don't know why, because I think if Jesus were on the earth today, he'd be a liberal. He certainly wouldn't be a George W. Bush Republican! If you don't believe it, read the Bible. If you can find anything in the Bible that puts Jesus forward as a Conservative well, I'd be amazed.

KW: I see a lot of values of Christianity in your political beliefs.

GL: Well, George W. Bush thought he had them too. I hope my values are consisted with Christianity. Historians like you will have to evaluate that. I hope that what you are saying is accurate. But George Bush left the office saying, "I'm glad I never compromised on my principles." I'm sure he takes his principles from the Bible and I am amazed because I don't think we're reading the same scripture.

KW: When you read the Bible it seems you have a progressive interpretation?

GL: Well, I suppose. Norman Vincent Peale was out of tune with the rest of the clergymen. When he started Positive Thinking, he was really frowned upon by a lot of the clergy. And I'm sure Robert Schuller is the same way.

KW: Dwight Eisenhower once said that you can't legislate morality, but you can legislate so that human behavior doesn't negatively impact other people.

GL: I think that's a good statement. I appreciate that. I don't think you can legislative morality. The state can certainly take a position on moral issues; taking care of children, keeping families together, providing for the needy. But it is human nature to do what we like to do, moral or not. Of course, some would say who defines morality? But Ike understood human nature and I think Ike understood that much of what is done by men—especially to women—is unconscionable and destructive to our society. I fully agree.

KW: Do you think you tried to regulate morality? Did you bring your own morals into what you put into law?

GL: Well I think every person in government brings his morals in if he or she has any. Sometimes I wonder. A lot of politicians, I think, in our major cities for example, are not immoral; they're amoral. They just don't have any moral standards. This is certainly true of some politicians that I won't name. They're totally 100 percent pragmatic, maybe even idealistic, but they lack morals. I think the problem in democracy is when the majority of people become so pragmatic that they really dominate every election. And they tend to elect very pragmatic people. I would say 90 percent of the United States Congress gets reelected every time. Nobody could tell me that all of them—that 90 percent of them—*deserve* to be reelected. Then they get the seniority. They get to chair the major committees and subcommittees. Then the government is no longer a force for good in the nation, but it's rather a place for the survival of people who want to be in politics all their lives. If we threw some of the people out down there that would be a good thing.

KW: Do you think some people want to be in politics for ego purposes?

GL: I think a lot of them have inflated egos. We talk about drug addicts and money addicts and sex addicts and gambling addicts; I think there are political addicts who get their total charge and satisfaction out of life by serving in a political office which they *feel* is a place of high honor. And yet, they are the very people that destroy the honor part of it.

They're addicts to power. Some of those people get power and they enjoy it. They enjoy having that pork-barrel spending to make them look good at home. It is especially ironic that many of the conservative Republicans, especially, love pork but yet they say they are for cutting government spending! I guess they want to cut government spending—but not for them—just for everybody else. They enjoy presenting those checks back home.

KW: Do you think that you ever became enamored by power?

GL: My whole life is motivated by reaching goals, even small goals. And, many of those goals have been about helping others. Maybe that sounds idealistic. But it is what motivates me; always has. Yesterday I went to Lebanon to arrange to buy used clothing and shoes to send to my orphanage in Ghana (see chapter 7, The Humanitarian). That was a very rewarding day for me because I was successful in finding that, successful in them finding a warehouse to put it until we can put it in a container in March and send it over to Ghana. We send a container or two to Ghana every year. This year we will send 1,200 pairs of shoes, clothing for at least 1,000 prisoners, clothing and shoes for at least 200 or 300 children, clothing and shoes for at least 400 or 500 women. Now that to me, that's a goal and very fulfilling. That means more to me than if I was elected to the Congress of the United States or county commissioner or judge. I don't know how any judge can go to bed at night and feel good about being party to an effort to send someone to be executed. I guess somebody has to do it in our system but I do not want to be the one to do it. That's the kind of power that doesn't appeal to me. I like power that can help people. Or there's the other kind of power that's to help yourself. That kind of power doesn't appeal to me in particular. It never did.

Governor Leader's mission work in Ghana, and his other humanitarian ventures, have reflected his values derived from Christianity and are an extension of his views expressed here. It is to his contributions as a humanitarian that we now turn.

Notes

1. Henry Leader, interview with Kenneth C. Wolensky, May 7, 2009, York, PA.
2. Michael Leader, David Leader, and Jane Leader Janezcak, interview with Kenneth C. Wolensky, May 27, 2009, Hershey, PA.
3. George M. Leader, interview with Kenneth C. Wolensky, April 17, 2009, Hershey, PA.

7

The Humanitarian

Among George Leader's proudest achievements is his role as a humanitarian. He doesn't define himself in those terms though he will accept the moniker as applied by others. He explains that what he is doing in his mission work is simply fulfilling his commitments as a Christian rooted in the biblical beliefs that man is to help man, especially the disenfranchised, the impoverished, children, and the persecuted.

His mission work has taken place in three areas. First, Ghana, with education, food, and clothing programs for the poor and imprisoned. Second, a program called Second Chance Ministries conducted inside Pennsylvania's state correctional institutions (SCIs). And, third, he was the main force behind a program in Harrisburg's inner city schools to provide computers to students and led a program called I Am College or Career Bound. The Leader children provide their interpretation for their father's continued proactive nature, especially as a humanitarian:

> JLJ:[1] Mother has told me several times that when she married Dad he was a very shy individual who, she thought, would be completely devoted to family and be a teacher. He would be a person behind the scenes. She thought that would be the ideal lifestyle for her. He was shy. Apparently he was a terrible orator! Mother said he used to pull newspaper clippings out of his pocket and read them to her or his family. He occasionally does that now but with much more flair and ability. Well, his shyness certainly didn't

extend into adulthood. Thinking about it, it is sort of a contradiction or, maybe, a remarkable note of the potential for progress of every human being. He grew into this person despite his shyness. He is gregarious and extroverted. His public life and mission work reflect these characteristics. He reflects his skills not only in politics and business but also in his humanitarian work.

David Leader: I have to say I really do believe—and this is something I think I share with my siblings—that he has some attention issues but he focuses them positively. I won't go so far as to say he's ADD, but I think that he has developed the most incredible compensating mechanism for ADD: a very high sense of urgency and hyper-focus. So he has a terrific need to complete things *now*. Some of that energy simply comes from the way his brain works. But I certainly believe that it helps him to keep attention and focus, especially with his characteristics of hyperfocus and lots of energy. I think we've all seen him many times want to solve a problem or pick up the phone before he's even fully digested the problem to implement the solution. That's Dad.

JLJ: But it works for him and he always says, "You know, Jane, if you make 90 decisions in a day and 80 of them are right, you're way ahead of the ballgame." You know, he's right. It is worth taking a risk and, maybe, making some wrong decisions along the way. It's true that most people have difficulty making decisions.

DL: I give my mother and father a tremendous amount of credit for their kindness to others and their openness to accept all points of view. For example, I could come home and say that I was gay and I have no doubt that neither one of my parents would kick me out or reject me in any way. They wouldn't love me any less. I know that for certain and my brother and sister would agree. I do think that the person that demonstrates it most effectively is my mother. She has been the rock or the place where you absolutely knew the unconditional love was there. She certainly influenced Dad a great deal. I recall an incident as a child when I got a ride in a car with a realtor in the Gladwyn area where I grew up. He must have been the father of a friend. That area was a fairly wealthy suburban community. Even back then, it was a nice suburban community and not very diverse. The realtor asked me if I could have a word with my father and have him talk to our neighbor down the street who was going to sell his home to somebody more diverse—might have been Jewish or Black. I knew that wasn't appropriate but I didn't know how my father would react exactly. And so I told the story to Dad and he said "Who told you that? I want to talk with him." He was angry enough that he was going to follow it up. And, he did. I don't know what came of it but Dad certainly wasn't quiet about it.

ML: That's unusual, especially for a person from York County. York County was—and is—probably was one of the most conservative areas in the state. He came out of York County, seven or eight generations in York County. You wouldn't have expected that from him. Maybe somebody from Philadelphia or Pittsburgh but not York County.

KW: Where did his drive and compassion come from, especially coming from a conservative culture?

DL: It was in his family. It could also simply be genetic. Guy Leader was a strong role model. Beulah Leader also, in quieter, softer ways.

JLJ: I think the entrepreneurial and the political influence was definitely from Guy. His dad was, of course, a state senator and a great entrepreneur. He had passion for political issues.

ML: Grandfather Leader was also a builder. He owned four farms and he was always building and enhancing the property. He was very moral. One of the reasons he stepped down as state senator after his second term was because he didn't like the ethics of the people—of some of the people he was associated with in Harrisburg. He certainly influenced Dad not only in politics and business, but to build for others as well.

JLJ: As a result of his upbringing Dad is openly capable of unconditional love for the masses, for the disenfranchised, for the special needs kids, for the African-American disenfranchised, for the gay population, for the oppressed anywhere. My mother is the same yet she does it one-on-one, quietly. She helps people one-on-one. She'll never be in a newspaper for doing it but she's really good at helping people behind the scenes. Dad, on the other hand, will talk about what he does but not in a boastful way. I think he tries to get the reaction and input of others. That's why he will talk about it. I admire that greatly. I admire both of them for what they do. Mom and Dad are fabulous role models for what we could do in the world and the community at large; mother was this great role model for what we could do in our families and in our relationships with our spouses.

If you look at his life from the time he was in his 30s and in government, he has always helped others. He helped special needs children get access to education. He pushed the state's first nursing home licensing acts. If you watch him through his lifetime, every decade he's helping disenfranchised people up to today where he started the prison ministry and the mission in Ghana. He did the college or career program and computers-in-the-classroom initiative for the kids of Harrisburg. He got into the business of assisted living because he wants seniors to live with dignity and respect. He's now going global! And you know, if I mention to him that somebody's in need, he'll say, "Contact the (Country Meadows) warehouse and we'll get them some furniture." You know, this reminds me when we adopted this little boy who was legally blind. I called my mother and said, "You did such a great job raising Fred. What would you tell me to do in terms of guidance and direction?" And she said, "Well, I can't take credit for Fred." Although she could, she was being modest. She said, "Your father is the one who made me send him to public kindergarten." She said, "I didn't want to because he was crying every morning before he had to go. But Daddy made me send him." He tried very hard to help him overcome his handicap in different ways. And as a result of going to public school it made a difference. Of course at that time it was highly unusual. He was the only handicapped, disabled child in our school district. Later on, he went on to Swarthmore College and graduated with two distinctions in math and economics. My mother felt that was a pivotal moment when my Dad really forced her to go outside what she wanted to do emotionally. He does that in life; gets beyond the human comfort zone. On my father's tombstone is a quote "The Essence of Life is Unconditional, Non-Judgemental Love." I really think he tries to live that out. So does my mother.

Mary Jane Leader confirms her children's views:

MJL:[2] He is always looking out for people that nobody cares about such as the mentally ill. When he was Governor the mental health issue probably created more buzz than anything else because people misunderstood the mentally ill. George felt that there were a lot of people in the mental hospitals that really should have had advice and counsel and maybe drugs to help them. He tried to show how many times if they were there for a couple years, nobody ever bothered to find out why there were there or whether they were checked on by doctors. He really felt that was so wrong. I don't know how that sat with the powers that be who were satisfied with the way things were. Right now he feels that we're putting people in prisons too quickly. Sometimes maybe they haven't done anything that was really intended to harm anybody seriously. A more lenient sentence might be in order. George is so opposed to putting people away if they can be rehabilitated. I believe that too. He feels that we should know a lot more about the person and their problems and help them to get back on track. He was and is always on the side of the Democratic Party that holds these views.

Governor Leader explains his mission work and his rationales for it.

KW: You have been or are very active in mission programs. Many people would say, "Well, you're 91 years old, you've done a great deal in your life. You're successful in politics; you've been successful as a business person. Why don't you just kick back and retire and relax, read books and go to Florida?" Why do you stay so busy? Why do you execute these ideas and lead mission initiatives?

GL:[3] I spend two, three, four hours a day on my projects on the telephone, writing, reading, and studying. I get bored if I don't have something to think about. I need to feed something into my mind to work on. Sometimes my family gets tired of hearing me talk about some of these things that mean so much to me because they don't have the same focus I have, which is understandable. Not that they don't have a lot of great ideas, but they may not be as intense as I am. I'm pretty intense about what I do. I see so many opportunities and issues that need to be addressed. I want to use my energy and my remaining years on this Earth in service to others. God willing, I will be able to accomplish what I set out to do. The work is never done, however. I am making, really, a small contribution to all of the social and people issues that need to be addressed. And when something good comes along I want to pursue it. Mostly, they are projects to help people in need. To make life more meaningful for them is an achievement.

KW: Can you explain your passion?

GL: I wish I knew. God must have intended it. I certainly didn't plan my life and say when I'm 91, I'm going to start a mission in Ghana. God must have had an idea he wanted to use me this way because certainly I can't take credit for it. My father had a first cousin, Charles Leader and his wife Bertha, who were in Sierra Leone right next to Ghana. These were both colonies of the British. Cousin Charles and his wife, Bertha, spent all their lives in Sierra Leone in mission work. They would go over there for three years and come back and go off of quinine that they had to take to prevent malaria. They'd raise some money and they'd always come to my father's farm. Mother would cook a nice dinner for them and Dad would give them a check for $100—no small change during the Depression. They'd come back every three years. I'll never forget the last time cousin Charles was there. He put his hand on my head and he said, "Guy, don't forget. This is the most important crop you're raising." He was a wonderful man.

KW: Did he influence you?

GL: He did. I remember it after all of these years. It certainly made an impression, didn't it? It made a marked impression. He was a great man. He was a really great man. He could have been anything he wanted to be. He was so talented, so dedicated, so focused, so positive. My father's cousin—Charles Leader.

Governor Leader further discussions his specific humanitarian efforts:

Ghana

KW: You are leading a significant mission program in Ghana. Explain your motivation and program.

GL:[4] I'm always searching for what my next project is going to be. My charitable project in Ghana right now, which I'm doing in association with Chaplain Douglas Yeboah-Awasi, who is formerly the head chaplain at SCI Chester and has dual citizenship in Ghana and the United States. Ghana is one of the poorest places on Earth. He said to me, "I promised God I am going to go back to Ghana as soon as I can and help my people. The first thing I want to do is to buy eleven acres of ground over there to grow some food for the prison." I said, "What's it going to cost you?" He said, "Three thousand dollars." I said, "I'll give you the three thousand dollars." And I did, but that was just the beginning. We bought land over there and it has brush and trees on it so we want to clear it off to grow food on it for children who are in his orphanage and for a prison of 1,000 people not far from the orphanage. The food supply to that prison is so small that in a 90-day sentence some of them can almost literally starve to death. There's no health care there; we hope to do some good in that regard. They don't give the prisoners any clothing; we're taking clothing there. There are three more prisons not too far away that I'd like to help with food and clothing. Also, we constructed a cement block plant from which to supply building materials for the orphanage, a school, and other infrastructure. I am purchasing a van for the orphanage. We are cutting trees and brush on land that we are farming. There we planted acres of yams but we don't waste the trees. We use them to make building products. They don't have those big sawmills like we do here. But they have men over there that are so skilled with chainsaws that they can make rafters out of those trees, so we will be doing that. Also, we have a well driller over there who has a compressor to clean out wells that are dead that can't function anymore—put new pumps on them. Clothing is being sent that I purchased from the Salvation Army. Some will go to the community, some to the orphanage, and some to the prison. Over 1,000 t-shirts are being sent and I am working on having shoes sent over as well. Many of the people over there don't have decent shoes or any shoes at all. You know Nike sells their shoes for about $120 a pair to poor people in the inner city who, many times, are taking some of their food money to buy a pair of shoes. Nike buys those shoes in China for $5 or $6 a pair and sells them here for $120 a pair! But people in Ghana can't get shoes at any price. In March of next year (2010) I will send a container to Ghana with clothing and shoes. We send one every year for $7,000. And we'll send probably 1,200 pairs of shoes, clothing for at least 1,000 prisoners, clothing and shoes for at least 200 or 300 children, clothing and shoes for at least 400 or 500 women. The next major project will be a clinic because Chaplain Douglas's wife is a nurse-practitioner. In a few years, she's going to go over there to start a clinic for children. In some of those communities over there conditions are bad. Health is very poor. It takes four hours to get a sick person to a decent hospital. Sometimes they die on the way to the hospital. There are five diseases in Ghana that kill more people than AIDS. Now the AIDS programs are wonderful, and I'm all for them. But there's malaria, pneumonia, tuberculosis, dysentery, and internal parasites. Those five kill more people than AIDS. In some communities the fatality rate among children is so bad that 50 percent of the children die before they reach the age of five. Now that to me, that's a goal. That's something real. It means more to me than if I were elected to the Congress of the United States, or county commissioner, or if I was a lawyer, or elected judge or governor again. I like power that can help people. You know, Ken, there's the type of power that's to help yourself; that kind of power doesn't appeal to me in particular.

KW; I know you have special concern for the women of Ghana.

GL: That's right. I started a microfinance business program that is growing in leaps and bounds. In other words, we provide women with small amounts of money to start businesses using skills they already possess. It could be in a craft, clothing making, food, or something like that. We lend women $25, $50, or $100 to help them get started in what they're doing to produce and sell a product. This program can have an amazing economic impact. If we can keep them growing the status of women would change substantially.

Israel

KW: On another humanitarian topic, you have remained very proactive in issues relating to Judaism and Israel. And, there is a forested area in Israel named the Leader Woodland. What can you tell me about your advocacy for these causes and the Leader Woodland?

GL:[5] Well I made a number of speeches during my time in office for Zionist causes, which wasn't unusual for liberal governors in those days. The people who were active in the Jewish National Fund and some of the other Jewish organizations—such as Bonds for Israel—those people appreciated the fact that even though I was a non-Jew I supported those causes. At one point, they said, "We would like to put on a drive for a large woodland in Israel and we would like to name it for you. We would like to honor at least 25 or 35 other mayors and senators and so forth in Pennsylvania at the same time." I was quite flattered. In other words, it was going to be a woodland that would honor people in office at the state and local level. So they involved 37 other political leaders in the Leader Woodland. That was about 1957. I took my family over there in 1965.

The Leader Woodland is on the outskirts of Jerusalem. And of course, everybody thinks of Israel as being one giant desert. Well there is a giant desert there, and Southern Israel is one giant desert. But, at Jerusalem, they get 40 inches of rainfall a year on the average. So when we got there, much to my surprise there were decorative trees around the edges and the Jerusalem Pine were ten and fifteen feet tall because Jerusalem gets 40 inches of rain a year. We average 44 inches of rain here in Pennsylvania. So, I'm very proud of that woodland. I have a picture which I took of my children and wife standing in front of the bronze plaque at the Leader Woodland. The Leader Woodland runs for 9 km around the outskirts of Jerusalem and ends very close to the memorial to the Holocaust. Anyone who visits that museum, which is the memorial to the Holocaust, will never, ever forget it because it breaks your heart.

Education

KW: There was another project you led several years ago in the Harrisburg City School District.

GL:[6] Yes, I started a college and career bound program. It was designed to engage students in learning about career possibilities and college opportunities. Also, I provided computers to the city schools to upgrade their technology. I wasn't at all pleased with the college and career program, however. There was a poor response. It's awfully hard to deal with adolescent boys. They don't study; the best educators around would be lucky if they graduate 25 percent of the students who start school in the inner cities. Now, they've got some new things that they're doing. I talked to the superintendent recently. They have some new things that they're doing. They're taking the young boys who are the most disruptive and difficult and putting them in special classes with two or three to a teacher. Some are graduating. They're not only graduating, they're getting into college. So, we do know what works, but it's very costly. I'm delighted that President Obama knows what works. The Secretary of Education for the United States who came out of Chicago knows what the problem is. That's one of the things that President Obama is going to focus on. And if he can solve the problem in the inner cities and start graduating up to 50 or 75 percent of the class as opposed to the 20 or 25 percent we're graduating now, it will be a miracle. And I think they can do it only because the President understands the problem and the Secretary of Education understands the problem. They know what has to be done.

I didn't continue the Harrisburg program long enough and didn't run close enough records to find out. But I don't think I had much success. The girls do better than the boys. I remember some years ago when I lived in the Philadelphia area, I was on the board of the Fellowship Commission that was to help minorities. At that time we were graduating in Philadelphia schools eight girls for every boy. I was also on the Board of Lincoln University at that time and we didn't have enough students to stay in business. It was a male school. We were down to 400 students and weren't generating enough income to keep the schools going. Then we made it co-educational and the student body jumped up to 1,150. From that time on we've done very well. But the reason they could get girls is that girls were finishing high school in Philadelphia and boys weren't. So I've been not too amused by some politicians who talk about what they're going to do for the inner city schools who have never experienced it and really don't know how tough a challenge it is.

KW: Governor, there's people out there who say, "Well, the inner city problems are problems of their own making. Those individuals really have got to solve their own problem. They should pull themselves up by their own bootstraps." There's a philosophy like that out there, especially in American society, but what you're doing runs counter to that.

GL: I think there's a middle ground. I think if somebody is drowning and you try to rescue them, if they can still kick a little bit to help you to pull them over to the shore or over to the side of the pool, it helps. I think it takes both. I think you've got to have a certain amount of willingness. I'm amazed how well a lot of the African American girls do in contrast to the boys. When I was pushing my program at the Harrisburg schools, I took a minister along with his little granddaughter. And I said to that school board 20 years ago, I said, "This little girl doesn't want to marry some dummy. This little girl is going to go to college. She wants to marry a college man. She's not going to marry a college man if they don't exist, if they're in prison when they should be in college." One of those ministers that I was working with back in those days said that the reason there are no fathers in the homes is because they are in prison. Sixty-one percent of children back in those days in the Harrisburg school were in single-parent homes and the reason there were no parent in the homes is that the fathers were in prison. That's where they were.

Prison Ministry

KW: Governor, you have supported and been at the forefront of a program with the Pennsylvania Department of Corrections to train inmates in a ministry program. Can you talk about that program?

GL:[7] That's right. A number of years ago I began working with Jim Law, a former inmate who turned his life around and is now a Christian minister. He became the president of Second Chance Ministries. Actually, we train inmates to become Christian mentors to their fellow inmates. Sometimes, I call them missionaries. We are training them in 22 of the 27 state correctional institutions. We also have a program in about ten of the county jails that are not part of the state system. Some of those are computer training programs, and some of them are missionary training programs. The idea is to turn people's lives around while they're in prison so that when they come out, instead of going back in again as 60 percent of them do in three years, they will stay out. Many of these young fellows are not unlike the inmates that we are trying to help in a prison in Ghana. They've got them packed like sardines in a can. Very overcrowded. They've lived a tough life, on the streets in many cases. They don't have a roof over their heads, they don't have a source of clothing, they don't have a place to get food, so they steal the food. They get involved in drugs sometimes to make money. Or, they are alcoholics. If they steal sooner or later they get caught and then wind up in prisons—mostly young men. Their lives are ruined. In this country, the people that go to prison because of drugs are young men, for the most part, young minority men. They are in and out for the rest of their lives. Sure, it may only be a two- or three-year sentence the first time, but after they're out in a short time they're back in again and again and again—for the rest of their lives. The reason I'm doing a missionary program in the prison is to try to give them a foundation in the Christian religion that will help them to keep out, even though it will be tough for them to stay out when they come out. They come out with a suit of clothes and $75 in their pocket, and they mostly don't have anybody to help them. More than half of them have been completely abandoned by their families because their families are disgusted with them. I hope my program can help turn some of them around and I think it has helped.

I've been told that inmates in Pennsylvania's system are fifty percent white and fifty percent Black or other minority. If you see a picture of my graduating classes from SCI Camp Hill, for example, I think it is at least 75 percent African American. I don't believe that our prisons are 50 percent minority and 50 percent majority white. I don't believe those figures, I'm sorry. My graduating classes, which are generally from 12 to 20, are always at least 75 or 80 percent black. So, who are we locking up? People who have traditionally been disadvantaged in so many ways.

Poetry

KW: I want to ask you about your poetry. You've written now two books of poetry. One is very extensive; the other one is a bit shorter, but no less substantive. Your poetry, in many ways, is about humanitarian issues. When and why did you start writing poetry?

GL: I didn't start writing any poetry until I was 71. It just never occurred to me to do it. And then every once in awhile, I would get an idea. Rev. Robert Schuller would say "the Lord put the idea in my head." Maybe he did in my case. I hope so. I would get an idea that I wanted to preserve and share, in many cases. So I would sit down, a lot of times on a Saturday morning when I didn't have anything on my schedule. I had free time. I'd sit down and I'd take that idea and prepare the first couple of lines in my head. The remarkable thing is that by the time I finished that first draft I invariably had five or six verses. Now, I never had it the way I wanted it the first time. Most of the poetry was drafted six or seven times and probably could have stood more work than that. But six or seven times was about as much as I was willing to give to it. If I could encapsulate an idea in six or seven verses of poetry I found satisfaction in that, both from the standpoint that I could refer back to it and the fact that I could share it. Now, I never had any idea when I started out that it was going to be a book. I used to incorporate some of that poetry in my speaking. People would say "Hey that poetry was pretty good. You ought to do a book." You told me that one time, Ken. Well, it was a nice compliment, but I didn't take it too seriously. But then, one time I said, "You know I bet I've got a hundred poems." Because I always gave those hand-drafted poems to my secretary who typed them and put them in a looseleaf binder. So I said, "Do you want to check?" She checked and found out that I had 250. So we did a book called *Healing Poems*. That was in my 70s. Then in my 80s, I started writing poetry again for the same reason, not thinking that I would ever get enough for another book. One day, I said, 'You know there must be a dozen poems in there now.' She counted them, and there were over 100. I said, 'Well we've got enough for another book.' In my 80s I published *Healing Poems II*. Now I'm in my 90s, and I have written very little since then. I don't know if I'll ever write that much poetry again. I'm not searching for poetry, but if I get up one morning and there's something in my head that appeals to me I might sit down and see what I can do with it. Now once in awhile, I'll have an idea that I can't do anything with. I'll give it a second try. If I can't make something out of it by the second try, I throw it away. But, most times, I can get something together on the first try.

KW: How does an idea come to you?

GL: I don't know.

KW: Give me an example.

GL: I don't know. I can't even give you an example. Usually on a Saturday morning I have some free time. My brain has to occupy free time. Now, I assume a poem will have something to do with something I've heard, or read, or seen. But I don't have a magic formula that I can just sit down and write a poem. The idea has to be in my head before I sit down.

KW: I think one of your favorite poems is *The Like-Wiser*.

GL: Yes. "Go and do likewise is truly what he said." It is about carrying out the message of Christianity in human affairs. It is also about the Good Samaritan. I wrote three poems based on the Good Samaritan in that first book.

KW: What are some of the other topics that you have written about?

GL: They mostly have a spiritual content. Some of them are about family or friends. Some are about subjects like homosexuality. I think mankind, including many clergymen, has been so cruel and inhumane to homosexuals. I wonder how many additional suicides we have amongst teenagers because they can't go to their parents and they can't go to their pastor or their priest and explain their lifestyle to them. There are a very large number of teenagers committing suicide. Some because of drugs or family problems. Others because they are homosexual and have no place to turn, no place to get support, no place to get love.

KW: Might also contribute to drug and alcohol problems—substance abuse?

GL: Yes, escapes. Any escape, even overeating. It's a hard thing to live with in a society that doesn't accept homosexuality. If you look around your extended family you are almost invariably going to find homosexuals. I know about four in our extended family. I pray for them. They should not be chastised for who they are.

KW: You are very *passionate* about such issues and I'm hearing compassion in your voice as well. Why are you so passionate?

GL: I guess it goes back to some of my Mennonite blood. My grandmother Leader came from a Mennonite family. That is part of our heritage. I've also had great admiration for William Penn and the Quakers. I said to a nice Quaker lady some years ago, "I think Quakerism is a wonderful religion." The woman's name was Eleanor Stabler Clark and she was the wife of my first boss in mortgage banking after I left the governorship. I said, "Mrs. Clark, almost all of the Quaker meeting houses in my part of the state—south central Pennsylvania—are either vacated or have very, very small congregations. Maybe a dozen people turn out on a Sunday." I said, "What happened to Quakerism?" One of her ancestors, I think, signed the Declaration of Independence. She was on the board of Swarthmore College and other Quaker institutions. I said, "What happened?" She said, "If you disagreed they would throw you out of the church," She said, "And they kept throwing people out until there was nobody left." I think she taught me one thing: Never exploit, or even explain too much about your difference of opinion on religion. Always consider the fact that the other person has the same right to his beliefs in religion that you have for yours in a free society. If we did it all that way, and we all just lived the best we could with the education we received from our religion, and the other person did the same thing, it would be a pretty good world. It would be a pretty good world.

KW: Isn't it unusual, by Pennsylvania German and Lutheran standards, to be a risk-taker and to be outspoken and to extend humanitarian efforts beyond one's own community?

GL: That's true. I know I am unusual in that regard. Pennsylvania Germans and Lutherans are a conservative people. As I've said, it must go back to some of the Mennonite and Brethren blood that came through my grandmother Leader. They were people who had great conviction. They were pacifists and went against the state religion—Catholicism. They did not follow the state religion and were persecuted for it. That is why many of them emigrated to the west. Those people in Switzerland were a special breed,

I think. As far as the Lutherans are concerned there were a few risk-takers. Martin Luther was certainly at the center of the highest order and took a risk for his very life and his livelihood when he nailed those things on the door of the church. I guess he set an example for me and, of course, my father's progressivism did as well.

When it comes to risk taking, it is simply part of George Leader's life and philosophy whether it's politics, business, or advocating correctional reform, promoting a mission program in Ghana, or other ventures. Moreover, he has little intention of slowing down.

Like her husband, Mary Jane has supported causes and programs that meet human needs. Her children are correct. While their father is more open and expressive about his humanitarian concerns, Mary Jane is much more private and quiet. For example, she has been an ardent supporter of C.A.R.E., a leading worldwide humanitarian organization aimed at fighting poverty, providing aid to those affected by war, and establishing basic health care and nutrition programs in severely impoverished areas:

KW: You are very supportive of the C.A.R.E. Why?

MJL:[8] It is a wonderful organization and they're very well managed with highly trained people. I've supported C.A.R.E. financially and morally. They have a tremendous mission to help people across the world that are affected by poverty. So many people suffer, you know. I am particularly sensitive to the needs of children. So many live in poverty in Africa and other places—right here in the United States. It isn't right, certainly not Christian to let this continue. On occasion, when a family member has gotten married, I've given a contribution to C.A.R.E. in their name.

U.S. and international philanthropic missions are very unusual when it comes to former Pennsylvania governors. George Leader and his family are unusual in this regard. Indeed, he stands alone as a former Pennsylvania governor who has invested in assisting the impoverished on the African continent and in assisting inmates in the state correctional institutions to redirect their lives. He concludes:

GL:[9] When I get up in the morning and maybe I'm remembering some wrong that somebody has done to me or somebody else, or somebody who is taking a selfish, greedy attitude towards mankind or their fellow man, if those things begin to bother me—and they do—I'll think of some good thing that I might do that day that will be positive. I find that good in my mission programs. My prayer every morning is: *God, Thank you for today. Help me be a blessing to someone, somewhere, somehow today.* And most days, God answers that prayer.

Notes

1. Michael Leader, David Leader, and Jane Janeczak Leader, interview with Kenneth C. Wolensky, May 27, 2009, Hershey, PA.
2. Mary Jane Leader, interview with Kenneth C. Wolensky, June 19, 2009, Hershey, PA.
3. George M. Leader, interview with Kenneth C. Wolensky, March 26, 2009, Hershey, PA.
4. George M. Leader, interview with Kenneth C. Wolensky, March 26, 2009, Hershey, PA.
5. George M. Leader, interview with Kenneth C. Wolensky, March 26, 2009, Hershey, PA.
6. George M. Leader, interview with Kenneth C. Wolensky, March 26, 2009, Hershey, PA.
7. George M. Leader, interview with Kenneth C. Wolensky, March 26, 2009, Hershey, PA.
8. Mary Jane Leader, interview with Kenneth C. Wolensky, June 29, 2009, Hershey, PA.
9. George M. Leader, interview with Kenneth C. Wolensky, March 26, 2009, Hershey, PA.

Epilogue

The twentieth century was a remarkable time in human history. Technologically, the century far exceeds any other in recorded human existence. And the inventions are breathtaking: the internal combustion engine; jet airplanes; nuclear fission and fusion; the computer that evolved from being the size of a substantial room to fitting on an ordinary desktop; and electronic microprocessors name just a very few of the technological marvels of the era.

Technology paired up with scientific advancements to achieve astonishing results as well. Rocketry; successful landings on the lunar surface; deep-space probes; satellites for all kinds of purposes; instantaneous electronically based mass communications from party-line telephones to cellular phones, right down to the popular iPods that children and teens are seldom seen without in the twenty-first century.

Likewise, treatment of human disease was greatly advanced. Significant diseases such as smallpox and polio were virtually eradicated. Inventions to treat cancer were developed in an era when the disease took on epidemic proportions. New diseases emerged, such as acquired immune deficiency syndrome or AIDS, and the response of public health institutions, scientists, treatment facilities, and physicians and hospitals were mobilized in what might well be the most organized medical effort in the shortest period of time to treat a deadly disease. The roles of diet, food, air, water, and the environment and their impact on disease and longevity were better understood to the point that federal and state legislation regulated industrial environmental abuses, conserved land, forests and ecosystems, and required that food products be labeled so that consumers know what they were eating. And, to fund human access to medicine a product called health insurance was developed and marketed by the public and private sectors, although equitable access to it remains a serious question.

In the Western world capitalism firmly took root in the twentieth century. Indeed, from the mid-nineteenth century to the mid-twentieth century it became clear that most of Western society was transforming from agrarianism to industrialism. Free enterprise coupled with mass production to create demand for growing consumer markets and to supply those demands. At least twice in the century the wisdom of the profit motive was seriously challenged nearly to the breaking point. The Great Depression that lasted from 1929 to about 1941 taught important lessons that, left to its own devices, free enterprise capitalism and the unregulated market was abusive, greedy, and reflected misplaced values. The public sector responded with legislation, regulation, and policy to ameliorate excesses and help those powerless against the vicissitudes of the private market. Societies and cultures change very slowly however. By the end of the twentieth century it was clear that capitalism hadn't been tamed and tens of millions faced hardship and financial ruin once again as the world economy faltered thanks mainly to loose credit, excessive corporate profits, and human greed. So-called government bailouts of corporations was the only answer to stave off worldwide economic depression in an economic crisis often referred to as the Great Recession.

Finally, on the human rights front the twentieth century was rife with change though it is apparent that much remains to be done. In the United States civil rights for African Americans, women, and other minorities and ethnic groups were legislatively guaranteed, though discrimination remains a very real part of American society. Human rights were protected, perhaps best exemplified by the United Nations' Declaration of Human Rights, although it often hasn't been respected. And, oppressive government regimes were challenged and some completely collapsed as evidenced by the defeat of Nazi Germany, Fascist Italy, and totalitarian Japan in the wake of the Second World War. The implosion of the Soviet Union in the early 1990s may serve as the quintessential example of how oppression eventually collapses on itself.

To conclude his biography in a final oral history interview on April 23, 2010, I asked Governor Leader several questions on his views of the tremendous economic, political, social, and cultural changes that he witnessed—and sometimes played a role in—during his lifetime. Governor Leader offers his reflections:

> KW: In your 92 years, you've seen a tremendous amount of change in the United States and the world. For example, when you were a youth the jet airplane didn't exist. Certainly the internet didn't exist and treatments for many diseases were rudimentary at best. When you think back on the many changes that you've seen—and some which you've been a part of—what comes to mind?
>
> GL:[1] Well I think it's a mixed blessing. I think some of the technological advances have served mankind well and some have not. I remember that I spent millions of dollars in taxpayer funding to put the first computers into the state government when I was in office. At that time we had about 70,000 people on the payroll. I thought that computerization was going to result in great savings on doing the payroll, budgeting, and other administrative tasks. Well, it turned out it took five years to get the payroll system operating correctly! I'm sure within five years the technology advanced so much that our state equipment was out of date. Today we are so dependent on computers. People spend hours and hours every day in front of a computer screen. I think that means that they communicate less face to face. I don't know if that is progress. As far as atomic bombs are concerned, we bankrupted Russia and right now the United States has twelve trillion dollars worth of debt, a good part of it building up our atomic bomb capabilities and for defense. Both Russia and ourselves have enough to destroy the entire world. Is that progress? I don't know how the military thinks. Someone said the military is always ready for the last war and never for the next one. We were ready for the last war and now the next war—our real war—is against terrorism. You can't kill terrorists with atomic—nuclear—bombs. So I say some of these advances have not been good. Now, about farming. When I was a boy, fifty percent of the people in America worked for agriculture, many of them on family farms. The nation's food supply was almost guaranteed

because it was scattered all over the nation in small holdings. Now you've got a few big conglomerates that own our farms. I don't think that it is progress to destroy the family farm and the livelihoods of those that depend on it. Consider that most of the country's tomatoes come from big corporate farms in Florida. If they have bad weather in Florida that pretty much wipes out our tomato supply. And they have had bad weather down there and the crops have been destroyed. So not all changes are advances; some of them are a mixed blessing. I have mixed emotions. I'm a liberal; I'm a progressive. I love a new idea. I go through fire to carry out a new idea; that's what makes my life exciting. But not all new ideas are good for mankind. Computers, nuclear technology and corporate farming are good examples.

KW: You have seen many advances in medicine in your lifetime.

GL: Yes. We have come a long way. My father always told us kids a story about a country doctor in York County. Back in those days a schoolteacher could get into medical school if he had any kind of a decent background. And our country doctor was a schoolteacher who went to Jefferson Medical School, which in those days—and still is—one of the finest medical schools in the country. When he graduated there were about five specific medicines he used to treat people. That's it. Five medicines. One was castor oil. He had ear drops for earaches. He had aspirin and one or two other medicines. Today there are probably thousands of medications. Just about one for any ailment. How many different kinds of antibiotics do we have, for example? How many different kinds of miracle drugs do we have? We are keeping people alive much longer, but we're also increasing the percentage of those people who, in their old age, develop dementia, Alzheimer's, and Parkinson's disease. So it's a blessing, yes. But is it a blessing to stay an extra ten years if you're suffering from Parkinson's or Alzheimer's disease or cancer? I don't know. My father said before he died, "I don't mind dying," he says, "but I don't want to be a vegetable." I share that feeling. I'm 92 years old. My dad lived to be almost 91. He had some physical problems. His mind was still clear. He was blessed by having a clear mind up until he was 91 years old. On a related matter, I think our greatest advances really may have been in animal breeding and plant breeding. Because when I was in the chicken business forty years ago, it took us twelve weeks to produce a three-and-a-half or three-and-three-quarters-pound broiler chicken. And, it took four pounds of feed for every pound of flesh on that bird. Today they're producing that size bird in eight weeks with two pounds of food. They cut the amount of feed in half; they cut the time factor to about two-thirds. Back in my day we didn't have the antibiotics for animals. I was called a chicken doctor, and I always had only a few drugs in the trunk of my car when I went out. I knew how to open up a chicken and see what was wrong with it. I would take a little bit of training in it, and I was pretty good at it. But today they're much more sophisticated, these big operations where they have maybe 50,000 or 100,000 in a broiler house and the feed is automatically dispensed and the water is automatic. If they need to put a drug in the feed or the water, they can put it right in at a moment's notice and keep the birds alive. They have a high percentage of livability. I saw something recently. Some of the flowers you see now in the spring were developed by the plant breeders. I called the School of Agriculture at Penn State about a year ago, and I was trying to press them to see what they're doing about making sugar beets available to grow in Pennsylvania. When I was governor, we didn't have soybeans in Pennsylvania. So I said to my secretary of agriculture who came off the faculty of Penn State, I said, "Dr. Henning, why don't we have soybeans here?" He said, "Well you can't bag them up. We don't have the processing plant here, so we can't grow them." Today, 50 years later, I look around the fields and at least a third of our fields are in soybeans. If I had been smart enough back 50 years ago to say "Dr. Henning, why don't you get somebody to *build* a soybean processing plant?" we'd have been all right. Now I'm calling Penn State a year ago about getting soybeans and sugar beets. Why? Because corn isn't what you want to make ethanol. Corn is very inefficient. If you use the sugar beets or sugarcane or soy, as they do in Brazil where they are now energy sufficient, it can produce a tremendous amount of ethanol. We can also take woodchips and make ethanol. Corn is not what we need. We're competing then with food products, and we're running the price of corn up that many of the nations can't afford it for human consumption. And, so, the School of Agriculture at Penn State is working on some plant breeding to produce ethanol.

KW: What do you think is the greatest or the most significant technological advancement that you've seen or experienced?

GL: I guess the use of uranium in generating power. That may be the most advanced thing we have now. On the other hand, I think the fact that we are now learning to capture the waves in the tides and the winds and the sun will help the United States and other countries to meet all of the energy we need now for civilization for years to come. The technology also exists to run our automobiles on hydrogen which sends no CO_2 into the sky. However, I can't believe that we're not moving faster in that direction. Of course now that oil is up to $83 a barrel and rising there will have to be some change in our gasoline consumption.

Governor Leader is a positive person. Seldom does he discuss his failures or disappointments in life. To conclude his biography I asked Governor Leader to reflect on such matters.

KW: I want to conclude by asking you, as you look back over your life, what do you think was your greatest disappointment?

GL: Well, my greatest failure was the fact that I think I was destined to be in government but didn't pursue such a career beyond being governor. I had the opportunity to run for governor again but never pursued it. I think maybe my greatest contribution to mankind *could* have been in government, had I continued to pursue elected office. Do I regret not doing it? Well, it's a very high price to pay. Someone said, "How is public life?" Well there's nothing wrong with public life, except that it completely destroys your private life. I have a wonderful family; I love them. They're hard-working, decent, honorable citizens. And I'm not sorry that I didn't continue to follow a public career. On the other hand, I didn't have a private fortune to fall back on. One of my friends in politics in my early days said, "George, never depend on politics for a livelihood." He said, "If you do, you'll die broke and brokenhearted." Well I don't plan to die broke or broken-hearted; although I'm doing my best to give my money away as fast as I can. I have much to be thankful for in having a wonderful family. But I think my greatest calling was to serve in government. And I think I made some sacrifices for that in my early career, but I sometimes have a guilt complex that I didn't continue longer.

For anyone who was born and lived in the twentieth century it has proven to be a remarkable time. At the beginning of the century few could have predicted the developments in technology, science, healthcare, and many other fields that characterized the century. And, the relatively small piece of land called the Commonwealth of Pennsylvania wasn't left out of these enormous developments. Its history attests that, in many ways, it even led the way.

Governing in this era, whether at the federal, state, or local level, often called for leadership, vision, and perseverance. It required *challenging complacency*. Leadership demanded that the status quo not remain if humanity was to advance. National leaders such as Woodrow Wilson, Franklin and Eleanor Roosevelt, and Lyndon Johnson, to name just a few, fit the bill and did their best to meet the challenges, though sometimes the nation fell well short.

In Pennsylvania it seems clear from history that vision hasn't always been the norm in public affairs though there have certainly been exceptions. Perhaps greatest among these exceptions was William Penn himself, whose vision of religious freedom and tolerance still stands as witness to the world that human life can be better. If we look to the twentieth century historians can find examples of vision in the Keystone State's political leaders. Gifford Pinchot, governor from 1923–1927 and 1931–1935, ranks at the top. Other governors and public sector leaders, all with apparent shortcomings, had vision as well. It is in this context that history can place George Michael Leader.

Historians evaluate the past based on various factors such as the context of the times in which events occurred, people lived, and events happened. They evaluate history by measuring the impact of human ideas and decisions and how those ideas and decisions affected humanity whether positively, negatively, or in some other fashion. Historians use place, artifacts, documents, oral testimonies, and other tools to evaluate the past. Then they use such tools to provide their interpretation of the meaning of people, places, and events.

History is not a perfect science. It is subject to human interpretation. For example, we may know that a certain event occurred at a certain place at a specific time. Examples might be the ratification of the U.S. Constitution in the late eighteenth century or the signing of the Emancipation Proclamation in 1863. However, what the event has meant and how it is interpreted is subject to the views of the interpreter. As one sees history another may completely disagree. One may provide evidence to support his or her interpretation while another can provide evidence to support an alternative point of view.

One interpretation of the evidence provided here is that Pennsylvania's gubernatorial administration from 1955–1959 had vision and challenged complacency. Moreover, George Leader's life, too, has challenged complacency. Human flaws and frailties are evident here as they are in all people. Perfection simply doesn't exist, nor can it ever be attained when in comes to human beings. Yet, with regard to this life, the evidence suggests that Leader worked to deal with the challenges of the times in a thoughtful and progressive way, to improve life especially for the disenfranchised, did not expect government to operate on cruise control, and worked to address human needs as best as he and his administration knew how. Such conclusions can be extended to his nongovernmental life as well. Indeed, these strivings sometimes fell short and other times achieved their intentions, but seldom lacked sincere effort. Complacency, after all, seldom yields without a tough challenge.

Note

1. George M. Leader, interview with Kenneth C. Wolensky, August 28, 2009, Hershey, PA.

Appendix A

George M. Leader Family Library and Archives, Master List and Finding Aid

Box 1

Military Service, George M. Leader and Official Photographs of Governorship, 1955–1959

Box 2

Personal and Family Photographs, Photographs from Trip to Israel, and *Pennsylvania Heritage* Magazine Articles, 2002

Box 3

Election and Inauguration, 1954

Box 4

Family Photo Albums

Box 5

Videos

Box 6

Leader and PA Cancer Crusade, *Time Magazine*, November 15, 1954

Box 8

Family Photo Albums

Box 9

Fred M. Leader Items, Business/Chicken Farms, William Penn High School, Family Albums

Box 10

Newspaper Articles, Albums from Governorship, 1955–1959, Inspirational Notations

Box 11

Family Cards and Photos, Mementos

Box 12

Videos and Family Photo Albums

Box 13

Patents of Walter S. Strickler, 1920–1960

Box 14

Patents of Walter S. Strickler, 1920–1960

Box 15

Inaugural Photos, 1954
Folders 1 and 1A: Inaugural Ball
Folders 2, 2A, and 2B: Swearing In
Folders 3, 3A, and 3B: Inaugural Parade
Folder 4, 1954: Gubernatorial Campaign

Box 16

Folders 1 and 1A: Mental Health and Hospital Tours
Folders 2, 2A, and 2B: Legislation Signings
Folder 3: Swearings-In of Cabinet and Other State Officials
Folders 4 and 4A: Ceremonial and Dedication/Ribbon Cutting Events

Box 17

Folder 1, 1A, and 1B: Ceremonial and Dedication/Ribbon Cutting Events
Folders 2 and 2A: Political and Public Events and Speeches
Folder 3: Personal and Family Photos

Box 18

Folder 1: Anthracite Region
Folder 2: Public Events
Folder 3: 1958 Flooding
Folder 4: Political Events and Speeches

Box 17

Oral History Interviews with Kenneth C. Wolensky, 2009 and 2010

George M. Leader
Mary Jane Leader
Henry Leader
Michael Leader
David Leader
Jane Leader Janeczek

Archives Organized and Arranged by
Aaron N. Wolensky
Kenneth C. Wolensky
with assistance from
Crystal Edwards

Appendix B

Manuscript Group 207
State Archives of Pennsylvania
Pennsylvania Historical and Museum Commission
George M. Leader Papers
1955–1959
504.5 cu. ft.

George M. Leader Papers 1955–1959 504.5 cu. ft.
Having served as chairman of the York County Democratic Committee and as a member of the Pennsylvania Senate, George M. Leader (b. 1918) was elected the Commonwealth's governor, 1954.

- Appointments, 1954–1959 (16 cartons) {#207m.1}
- General Files, 1955–1959 (84 cartons) {#207m.2}
- Legislative Files, 1955–1957 (26 cartons) {#207m.3}
- Miscellaneous, 1955–1959 (2 cartons) {#207m.4}
- Press Releases, 1954–1959 (17 cartons) {#207m.5}
- Subject File, 1955–1959 (53 cartons) {#207m.6}
- The container listings for this Manuscript Group are available for viewing and word-searching in PDF format:
  - [Holdings (part 1)]
  - [Holdings (part 2)]
  - [Holdings (part 3)]
  - [Holdings (part 4)]
  - [Holdings (part 5)]
  - [Holdings (part 6)]
  - [Holdings (part 7)]
  - [Holdings (part 8)]

Used with Permission from the State Archives.

Index

Achenbach, Jesse, 116
Anderson, Greg, 5, 119–22, 123

Bard, Judge Guy, 44, 45
Barr, Joseph, 115
Beck, David, 106
Beitscher, Henry, 52
Biddle, Anthony J. Drexel, 82–83
Blatt, Genevieve, 44, 45, 59, 69–70
Boehm, Charles, 55
Bradley, Andrew, 77
Bryan, William Jennings, 19
Bush, President George, W., 152

Cancer Recovery Foundation of America, 121
Casey, Governor Robert P. 4, 51, 56, 68
Castro, Fidel, 106
Clark, Senator Joseph, 2, 51, 108, 148
Clinton, Hillary-Rodham, 130
Clinton, President William J., 141
Country Meadows Retirement Communities 3, 114, 117, 122, 133–34
Cuban Missile Crisis, 86

Dewey, Governor Thomas, 36
Dilworth, Richardson, 45, 48, 59
Dirle, Louis, 52
Douglas, Senator Paul, 105
Duff, Governor James, 44

Earle, Governor George, 2, 51, 90
Eisenhower, Milton, 70
Eisenhower, President Dwight, 44, 54, 59, 80, 153
Ertel, Allen 107, 115

Fine, Governor John, 43, 47, 62
Finnegan, James, 45, 148
Flaherty, Pete, 107
Flood, Congressman Daniel J., 105
Flood-Douglas Area Redevelopment Act, 104
Fumo, State Senator Vincent, 149
Furman, Roy, 52

George M. Leader Family Library and Archives, 179–82
G.I. Bill of Rights, 110
Glen Rock Manufacturing Company, 13

Goddard, Maurice, 69–72
Greenfield, Senator Albert, 76
Guffey, Senator Joseph, 36

Haas, Francis, 55
Henning, William, 74, 175
Hoffa, James, R., 105–6
Hoffman, Bob, 13
Hoover, J. Edgar, 104

International Ladies Garment Workers Union, 53

Janeczek, Lane Leader, 4, 115, 128, 129–31, 140, 155–57
Janeczek, Ted, 128, 129
Johnson, President Lyndon, 76, 108, 146, 148–49, 177

Kennedy, President John F., 104 146–47, 148
Kennedy, Robert F., 105

Lanius, State Senator, 20
Lawrence, Governor David, 51, 90–91, 101–3, 106, 109
Law, James, 165
Leader, Alex, 129
Leader, Andrew, 129
Leader, Bertha, 160
Leader, Beulah Boyer 1, 17–18, 54, 157
Leader, Catia, 129
Leader, Charles, 160
Leader, David, 4, 115, 128, 129, 133, 140, 156–57
Leader, Frederick, 11–12, 77
Leader, Frederick, 4, 128, 129, 131–32
Leader, George Michael III, 4, 54, 115, 116, 128, 129, 133–35, 139–40, 157

Leader, George Michael IV, 129
Leader, Governor George Michael: abortion, 83–84; at Gettysburg College, 1, 26–27; at University of Pennsylvania, 1, 27; campaign for governor, 1954, 60–61, 122; campaign for state treasurer 1952, 45–46; campaign for U.S. Senate, 102–7; Civil Service reforms, 57, 61–62; community colleges, 85–88; early life, 16–25; education for disabled children, 77–78; election to State Senate, 43; entry into long-term care industry, 112; environmental policies and programs, 57, 68–74; equal property rights for women, 85–86; Fair Employment Practices Commission, 56, 75–78; family and children, 128–35; Ghana mission work, 153, 160–62; graduated income tax proposal, 63–64; Harrisburg City Schools Program, 163–64; Hiram G. Andrews Vocational Rehabilitation Center, 57, 79; inauguration as governor, 54; in *Time* magazine, 53; in World War II, 38–41; mental health reforms, 57, 65–68; opportunities to work in Kennedy and Johnson administrations, 108; opportunity to work for Penn Central Railroad in bankruptcy, 109; Pennsylvania Industrial Development Authority, 57, 63–65, 105, 110; poetry, 4, 166–68; poliomyelitis vaccination program, 78–79; political philosophy of, 140–41; political views, 149–54; Second Chance Ministries, 143–44, 165–66;

transportation infrastructure, 57, 81, 83; views on Adlai Stevenson, 147–48; views on corrections and the prison system, 144–45; views on education, 163–64; views on John F. Kennedy, 146; views on Lyndon Johnson, 146–49; views on Israel, 162–63
Leader, Grace, 129
Leader, Guy, Jr. 14, 20, 27
Leader, Guy, 1, 2, 13–15, 18–20, 27, 54, 122–23, 139–40, 157
Leider, Heinrich, 11
Leader, Henry, 14, 20, 27, 59, 60, 66, 77, 138–39
Leader, Jean, 14, 20
Leader, Jennifer, 129
Leader, Karen, 129
Leader, Katelyn, 129
Leader, Kristin, 129
Leader, Kyle Lee, 129
Leader, Liesa Hall, 129
Leader, Lois, 14, 20
Leader, Manuel, 129
Leader, Mary, 14, 16, 20
Leader, Mary Jane, 1, 54, 92, 111, 114, 119, 121, 126, 127–28, 129, 130, 134, 155–56, 158–59, 169–70; courtship with George M. Leader, 28–31; during World War II, 41–42; early business ventures with George M. Leader, 42; gubernatorial campaign of 1954, 48–49; marriage to George M. Leader, 31
Leader, Meredith, 129
Leader Nursing and Rehabilitation Centers, 109, 114, 134
Leader, Paul, 14, 16, 20
Leader, Ricardo, 129
Leader, Tania, 129

Lewis, Sam, 44
Love, George, 44

Martin, Governor Edward, 36, 44, 45, 102
Mattison, Berwyn, 55, McCarthy, Senator Joseph, 43
McGonigle, Arthur, 102
Mellon, Richard, 82–83
Menges, Congressman Frank, 125–26
Mondale, Walter F., 116
Musmanno, Michael, 47
Myers, Senator Frank, 36, 148–49

Nixon, President Richard, 4

Obama, President Barack, 130, 164
Office of Economic Opportunity, U.S. Department of Commerce, 105

Peale, Norman Vincent, 123–24, 152
Penchan, State Senator Albert, 43
Penn Central Railroad, 109
Pennsylvania Farm Show, 15
Pennsylvania National Guard, 87
Pennsylvania Railroad, 60
Pennsylvania State Archives, 6
Penrose, Boise, 59
Pinchot, Cornelia, 72
Pinchot, Gifford Bryce, 72
Pinchot, Governor Gifford, 5, 21–22, 56, 59, 62, 68, 74, 138, 141, 151
Prasse, Arthur, 72
Providence Place Retirement Communities, 3, 6, 111, 117, 134

Reagan, President Ronald, 116
Roosevelt, Eleanor, 177

Roosevelt, President Franklin, 2, 20, 21, 36, 90, 138–39, 146, 177
Ross, F. Clair, 36

Salk, Jonas, 79–80
Schlesinger, Arthur, 148
Schuller, Robert, 121, 123, 152
Scott, Senator Hugh, 102–7
Scranton, Governor William, 1, 46
Shafer, Governor Raymond, 68, 83
Shapiro, Harry, 5, 65, 112
Shapp, Governor Milton, 5, 51, 56
Sordoni, Senator Andrew, 77
Soviet Union, 86–88, 105, 173
Stevenson, Adlai, 44, 47, 147–48
Swan, Ralph, 55

Thornburgh, Governor Richard, 110, 115
Truman, President Harry, 21, 146

United Mine Workers of America, 90

Wilbar, Charles, 55
Willkie, Wendall, 36
Wilson, President Woodrow, 177
Wood, Lieutenant Governor Lloyd, 2

Yaboah-Awasi, Douglas, 160
York Fair, 15

About the Author

Dr. Kenneth C. Wolensky is a historian and graduate of the Pennsylvania State University. He writes and speaks on Pennsylvania's political, social, industrial, and labor history. He was long associated with the Pennsylvania Historical and Museum Commission, Harrisburg, and teaches at Penn State. He is vice president of the board of the Pennsylvania Historical Association and serves on the board of the Pennsylvania Labor History Society.